AF600658

THE JUDICIAL POWER OF THE CHURCH

CANON 1553, § 1

THE CATHOLIC UNIVERSITY OF AMERICA
CANON LAW STUDIES
No. 337

The Judicial Power of the Church

CANON 1553, § 1

A DISSERTATION

SUBMITTED TO THE FACULTY OF THE SCHOOL OF CANON LAW OF THE CATHOLIC UNIVERSITY OF AMERICA IN PARTIAL FULFILLMENT OF THE REQUIREMENTS FOR THE DEGREE OF DOCTOR OF CANON LAW

BY

REV. JOHN ROHAN BOURQUE, S.T.L., J.C.L.
PRIEST OF THE DIOCESE OF SPRINGFIELD, MASSACHUSETTS

THE CATHOLIC UNIVERSITY OF AMERICA PRESS
WASHINGTON, D. C.
1953

Nihil Obstat:
EDUARDUS G. ROELKER, S.T.D., J.C.D.,
Censor Deputatus

Washingtonii, D. C., die I Maii 1953

Imprimatur:
CHRISTOPHORUS J. WELDON, D.D.,
Episcopus Campifontis

Campifonti, die XI Maii 1953

GIBSON BROTHERS—WASHINGTON, D. C.
PRINTED IN THE UNITED STATES OF AMERICA

6

CHRISTO
IUDICI MISERICORDIAE
ET
MARIAE
ADVOCATAE NOSTRAE

TABLE OF CONTENTS

Contents

PART II

LEGISLATION OF THE PRESENT DAY

FOREWORD

Judicial power, or the authority to settle disputes and to bring wrong-doers to justice, is a vital function in the government of the Church. Were the civil courts to settle ecclesiastical disputes, such as those which concern administration in the Church and the administering of the sacraments, and to determine the interpretation and application of ecclesiastical law to individual questions, there would be a serious deterrent to religious freedom. Indeed, were the Church unable to enforce its laws by trying and punishing those who violate them, there would be no such thing as discipline in religious society. As in every society, therefore, judicial power is an essential and integral function of the government of the Church.

The Church claims this right of judicial power, and enunciates the principles which determine its object and scope, in the first paragraph of canon 1553 of the *Code of Canon Law*,[1] and it is this canon which is the object of this dissertation.

It is to be noted that while this canon is incorporated in the Canon Law of the Church, it pertains not so much to the rights and duties of the members of the Church as to the constitution of the Church and its rights in regard to other juridically perfect societies, namely, civil governments. This canon pertains more properly, then, to public ecclesiastical law.

This dissertation accordingly is a study in public ecclesiastical law. It looks to the nature of the judicial power of the Church, its origins, the character of its authority, its function and objects, its

[1] Canon 1553, § 1. "Ecclesia iure proprio et exclusivo cognoscit: 1°. De causis quae respiciunt res spirituales et spiritualibus adnexas; 2°. De violatione legum ecclesiasticarum deque omnibus in quibus inest ratio peccati, quod attinet ad culpae definitionem et poenarum ecclesiasticarum irrogationem; 3°. De omnibus causis sive contentiosis sive criminalibus quae respiciunt personas privilegio fori gaudentes ad normam can. 120, 614, 680."—*Codex Iuris Canonici, Pii X Pontificis Maximi iussu digestus, Benedicti Papae XV auctoritate promulgatus* (Romae: Typis Polyglottis Vaticanis, 1917). (Hereafter all passages will be cited according to the canon of which they form part).

independence from, and correlation with, the corresponding judicial function of the civil society.

This work treats first of the influence of history, which brought a clarifying expression of the principles involved in the basic, functional relationship between Church and State. Then it deals with the present-day legislation, which crystallizes the teachings and experience of history concerning the nature of this power and its detailed correlation with the civil authority.

The Church-State relationship is, today, the subject of ponderous writings and bitter controversies. The divine plan, by which men in their spiritual and temporal needs are to be ruled by two distinct, but complementary, authorities and societies, has been distorted by the religious anarchy and excessive nationalism of the sixteenth century, and blurred and clouded almost beyond recognition by the militant atheism and Rome-fearing bigotry which have followed. Since judicial power is vital and essential to both societies, it is hoped that a study of the history of the judicial power of the Church concerning its origin in the positive divine law, and its functions under the totally divergent historical backdrops of persecution, of establishment, and of secularism, and of the careful respect which the legislation of the Church gives to the command of its divine Founder to render unto God the things that are God's, and unto Caesar the things that are Caesar's, will serve both to point out the divine nature and spiritual character of the authority of the Church, and to allay the needless and groundless fears of those who erroneously believe the Church to have any design upon the usurpation of civil functions and authority.

The writer wishes to express his gratitude to His Excellency, the Most Reverend Christopher J. Weldon, Bishop of Springfield, for making the pursuit of the present study possible; to the members of the Canon Law Faculty of the Catholic University of America, for their assistance with this dissertation and with the study of Canon Law in general; to his mother and father; and to those treasured friends and relatives without whose assistance and encouragement this work could never have been completed.

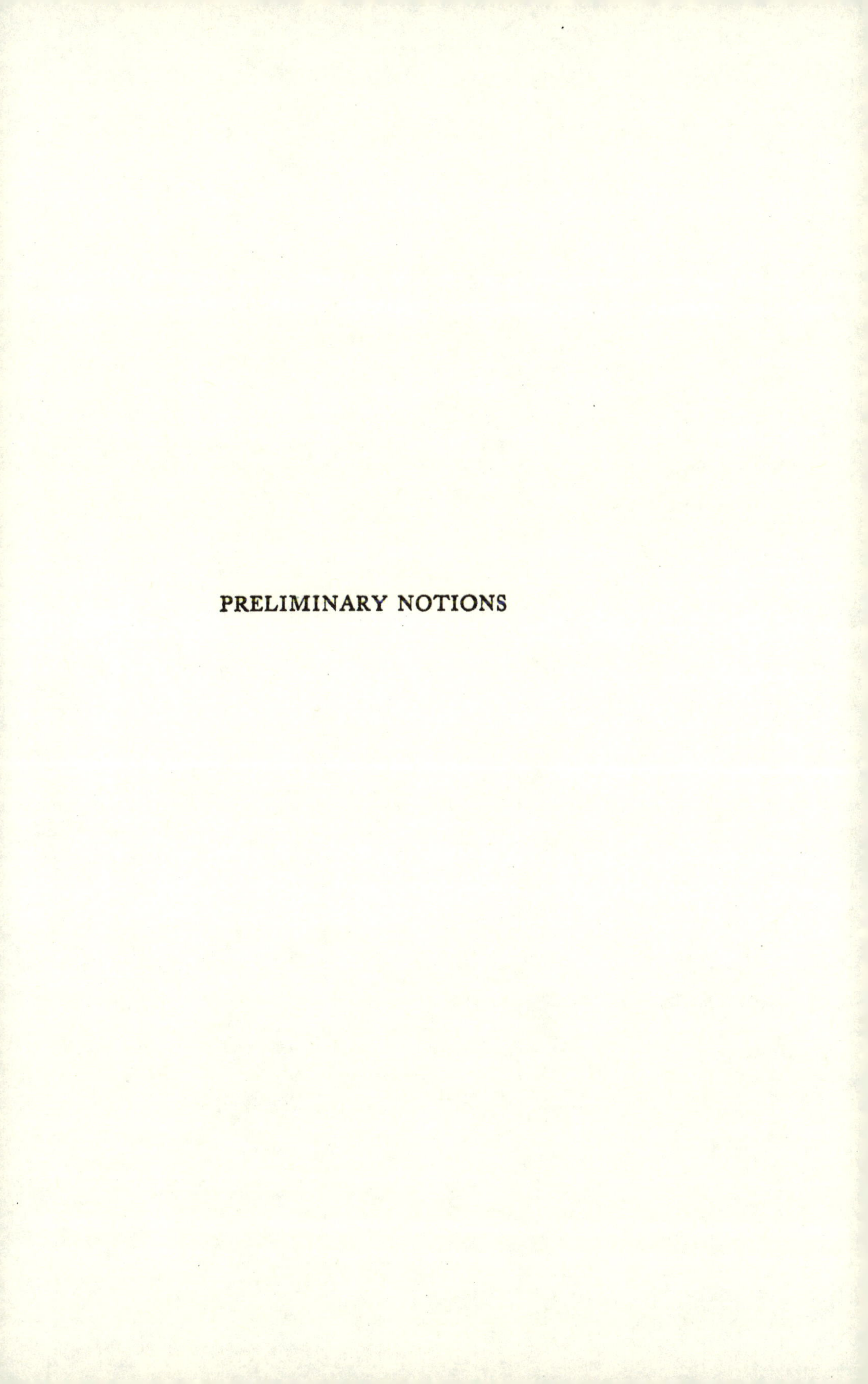

PRELIMINARY NOTIONS

CHAPTER I

PRELIMINARY NOTIONS

A. *Concept of Judicial Power*

Since human nature is limited in such a way as to prevent men from attaining the fulfillment of their lives by their own individual powers, they achieve the integration of their potentialities by means of co-operation with others,[1] and this concerted action, organized to achieve a common end otherwise unattainable by the individual, is the basis, the final causality, for those fixed and abiding associations among men which are called societies.[2]

The collectiveness of their activity, however, in no way destroys its human character.[3] It too needs an intelligence and a will capable of giving its direction, capable of efficiently moving it towards the common welfare. The agent which fulfills this need and function is called social authority, or government.[4]

The task of the social authority is like that of an architect. The work of the architect does not cease with the completion of his

[1] Cf. Messner, *Social Ethics* (Saint Louis, Mo.: B. Herder Book Co., 1949), p. 101.

[2] Society is defined as: "Plurium hominum unio ad eundem finem communibus mediis consequendum."—Ottaviani, *Compendium Iuris Publici Ecclesiastici* (2. ed. Romae: apud Custodiam Librariam Pontificii Instituti Utriusque Iuris, 1948), n. 6 (hereafter cited *Compendium*).

[3] Cf. Lottin, *Principes de Morale* (2 vols., Louvain: Editions de l'Abbaye de Mont Cesar, 1947), I, 61-75, where the author applies the Thomistic psychology of the human act to the act of social legislation.

[4] Leo XIII, ep. encycl. *Immortale Dei,* Nov. 1, 1885: "But as no society can hold together unless some one be over all, directing all to strive earnestly for the common good, every civilized community must have a ruling authority."—*Codicis Iuris Canonici Fontes* cura Emi. Card. Gasparri editi, 9 vols. (Romae [later Civitate Vaticana]: Typis Polyglottis Vaticanis, 1923-1939), n. 592 (hereafter cited *Fontes*), translation from *The Catholic Mind* (New York: The America Press), Vol. XXXIV, No. 21, November 8, 1936.

drawings and the commission of the builder or contractor. Though the builder directs the men, buys the material, and executes the plan, the architect, if he wishes to insure the realization of his design, must constantly check the accuracy and honesty of the work with the specifications, and must be available to interpret his drawings should any question or ambiguity arise.

In the same manner, the work of the social authority does not cease with the promulgation of those general directions, called laws, which are to lead the society intelligently to the attainment of the common welfare, nor even with the work of the executive power, in which, like the builder, it seeks to put these laws into execution. In order to collate the activity of all members of the society towards the common obective, it is necessary to apply the law to concrete cases, judging and settling difficulties, disputes, irregularities, and legal questions as they arise.

In other words, since the social authority is charged with the accomplishment of the common good through a co-operative act, which is no less human because of its collective character, it must find in itself all of the integral steps of a human act. But Saint Thomas Aquinas (1225-1274) found that it was not enough for the intellect to give a general direction ordaining all means to the goal which is sought (*imperium*), nor for the will to set about actually employing the means to the end (*usus activus*), but the intellect has to function in a continual supervisory and directive capacity over the work until the end is achieved (*usus passivus,* or *adeptio finis*).[5]

[5] St. Thomas breaks the human act down into the following twelve component acts of intellect and will:

ACTUS INTELLECTUS	ACTUS VOLUNTATIS
1. intellectus (apprehensio finis)	2. voluntas
3. judicium	4. intentio
5. consilium	6. consensus
7. judicium practicum	8. electio
9. imperium	10. usus activus
11. usus passivus (adeptio finis)	12. fruitio

"Ostensum est autem quod voluntas est quae movet potentias animae ad suos actus; et hoc est applicare eas ad operationem. Unde manifestum est quod *uti* primo et principaliter est voluntatis tanquam primi moventis; rationis autem tamquam dirigentis."—*Summa Theologica* (5 vols., Taurini: Marietti, 1932), Ia-IIae, q. 16, a. 1.

Accordingly the governing social authority has three distinct, necessary, and integral functions. Besides the legislative power, which directs all the means to the common end (*imperium*), and the executive power, which, with its governing, administrating and co-active functions, operates like the will to achieve the goal (*usus activus*), there must exist a supervisory agency to insure conformity of the acts of the members of the society to the legal order (*usus passivus*), which is precisely the function of the judicial power of society. Judicial power, then, takes its place as an essential part and necessary function of all social government.[6]

Judicial power is commonly defined by ecclesiastical jurists as "the right of declaring or pronouncing in an obligatory fashion what actions of one's subjects are, in the concrete, in conformity, and what are at variance, with the law, and the legal effects of this conformity or variance." [7]

Ultimately aiming at placing, or restoring, order in the world, which has been created by the wisdom of God in order and for order,[8] the immediate objects of judicial power are the prosecution or vindication of the rights of physical or moral persons, or the declaration of juridical facts concerning such persons, and the punitive or remedial punishment of delicts or crimes.[9] Hence the judiciary functions and judicial trials are of two types, contentious and criminal. The former is concerned with justice by the settlement of controverted

---

[6] Cf. Pius XII, Allocution to the Sacred Roman Rota, Oct. 2, 1945—*Acta Apostolicae Sedis, Commentarium Officiale* (Romae, 1909—), XXXVII (1945), 256 (hereafter cited *AAS*); Bouscaren, *Canon Law Digest* (2 vols., and Supplement through 1948, Milwaukee: Bruce Publishing Co., Vol. I, 1934; Vol. II, 1943; Supplement, 1949), Supplement, p. 208 (hereafter cited Bouscaren).

[7] "Ius declarandi seu proponendi modo obligatorio, quaenam subditorum actiones sint iuri conformes, quaeque eidem difformes, et effectus legitimos conformitatis aut difformitatis."—This is the definition given by Ottaviani, *Institutiones Iuris Publici Ecclesiastici* (3. ed., 2 vols., Civitate Vaticana: Typis Polyglottis Vaticanis, 1947), I, 92, as also by Tarquini, Cavagnis, Cappello, and Marchesi.

[8] Cf. Pius XII, Allocutions to the Sacred Roman Rota, Oct. 29, 1947,—*AAS,* XXXIX (1947), 496; Bouscaren, Supplement, p. 217; Oct. 2, 1945—*AAS*, XXXVII (1945), 256-9; Bouscaren, Supplement, pp. 207-8.

[9] Can. 1552, § 2.

rights among individuals, the latter with the protection and restoration of public order and tranquillity by declaring and inflicting punishment.[10]

The judgment of judicial power revolves about the juxtaposition and comparison of the law with a given set of circumstances and facts, and the intellectual assent or decision by the competent authority as to whether or not they coincide or conflict.[11] The primary task facing the court is to examine the facts of the case, and to judge, or decide, as to their conformity with, or violation of, the law. In performing this duty the judge may find himself faced with a case never contemplated in the law. Indeed, if the acts of men were always in open and apparent conformity or conflict with the law, there would be little use for judges and jurists, since the execution of the sentence, and the actual punishment of the culprit pertain to the executive, rather than to the judicial, function of government.[12] The judge, then, is obliged to interpret or supply for these ambiguities and gaps in the law. In this event, however, the judicial decision is authentic and binding only for the litigation at issue, and sets no precedent for further decisions on the principle of *stare decisis*.[13]

---

[10] Cf. Roberti, *Iuris Processualis Compendium* (2 vols., Romae: apud Custodiam Librariam Pontificii Instituti Utriusque Iuris, 194(?)), I, n. 27.

[11] Five constituitive elements are implied in judicial power: a) a hearing or discussion concerning a legal controversy or delict (trial, judicial procedure, action); b) contained in a formal charge or petition (implying a plaintiff); c) brought against some one (defendant); d) and an obligatory pronouncement as to what is due in law (sentence); e) rendered by a legitimately constituted person who is the agent of the social authority (judge, court). Cf. Bouix, *Tractatus de Iudiciis Ecclesiasticis* (2 vols. in 1, 3. ed., Parisiis, 1855), I, 6-14; cf. Roberti, *op. cit.,* I, n. 16.

[12] Cf. Roberti, *op. cit.,* I, n. 18.

[13] Cans. 17, § 1, § 3; 20. Cf. Cicognani, *Commentarium ad Primum Librum Codicis Iuris Canonici* (Romae: ex Officinia Typographica Romana "Buona Stampa," 1939), pp. 323-40; Cicognani, *Canon Law* (2. ed., English Version by O'Hara and Brennan, Westminster: Newman, 1935), pp. 597-607; 620-5. In this respect ecclesiastical judicial power differs from the practice of civil law, for in civil law, whether the law to be applied is taken from a constitution, from a statute, or from the common law, the precedent of former constant and concordant judicial decisions "is to be considered as part of the enacted law," (Smith, *Handbook of Elementary Law,* Hornbook Series

The judgment is the end-product of a process of reasoning which is formalized in a procedure called a trial. It is defined as the legal discussion and settlement before a tribunal of a controversy, in an affair over which the judge, or court, has jurisdiction.[14] Its principal elements are "a petition for the introduction of the case, a summons, the examination of witnesses, the communication of documents, the questioning of the parties, the termination of the trial, the judgment, the right of appeal." [15] The decision is embodied in the legitimate and binding pronouncement called the sentence. This sentence not only defines the controversy, absolving or condemning the defendant and answering all the doubts involved, but it also determines what the condemned person must give, do, suffer, undertake, or abstain from, in order to preserve or repair justice.[16]

Although social authority, or the right to rule, cannot be conceived as something divisible or separable, since such a division would frustrate the coordination necessary to obtain the common welfare, the diverse functions of this authority can be considered separately, and even delegated by the ruling power to different men or agencies.[17] In its concept, judicial power is quite distinct from legislative power. Its purpose is not that of making laws for the general community, but of applying the law to a given case. It is, therefore, correlative to, but supplementary of, and consequent upon, the act of the legislator. It is distinct from executive power because its authority begins with the summoning of the defendant, and ends with the rendering of the sentence. Except for a modicum of coercive power to insure the orderly conduct of the trial, it depends upon the executive to investigate a case and bring it before the court, to make arrests, and

---

St. Paul, Minn.: West Publishing Co., 1939, p. 83), and the principle of "*stare decisis* is at least the every-day working rule of our civil law," (Former Chief Justice Benjamin Cardozo, in a series of lectures given at Yale in 1921, entitled, "Nature of the Judicial Process," reprinted in *Cardozo, Selected Writings* [edited by Hall, New York: Fallon Law Book Co., 1947], pp. 107-84).

14 Can. 1552, § 1.

15 Pius XII, Allocution to the Sacred Roman Rota, Oct. 2, 1945—*AAS,* XXXVII (1945), 256, Bouscaren, Supplement, p. 207.

16 Cans. 1868; 1873.

17 Coronata, *Ius Publicum Ecclesiasticum* (3. ed., Romae: Marietti, 1948), n. 58.

to enforce its decisions.[18] Again, its decisions are neither merely consultative nor advisory, but authentic and obligatory. It differs, therefore, from both mediation and arbitration, because it is not voluntary and private, but authoritative and public.

The Sacred Congregations of the Holy See, like the executive bureaus of the civil government, exercise an administrative rather than a judicial activity, though often both its procedure and its effects lend a quasi-judicial appearance to their activity, as in the handling of *ratum non-consummatum* cases. The administrative process is distinct from the judicial process, however, in the purposes for which it is undertaken. The administrative process does not tend directly and immediately to the settlement of controverted rights between individuals, nor to the punishment of public delicts, though these effects may indeed follow. It is intent, rather, upon the orderly care and administration of one of the goods of the society which has been entrusted to its supervision. The Sacred Congregation of the Sacraments, for instance, may establish the rights or duties of an individual in regard to some sacrament, but its main objective is to protect the sanctity of the sacrament itself. Similarly the Federal Bureau of Communications may hold hearings for the purpose of allotting television channels, which procedure may have many characteristics of a judicial process, but its main concern is not the interest of the individual applicants, but the orderly administration of public communications.[19]

Though every society must have a governing, and hence a judicial, agent, the authority and force of that agent will correspond to the legal basis upon which the society is founded, and will therefore differ profoundly from society to society. Societies may be fraternal

[18] The judiciary possesses this coercive power in conformity with the principle that whoever has delegated authority is considered to possess also everything apart from which he could not perform his duty (can. 200, § 1). The judge exercises this power over the members of the tribunal (can. 1625, § 3), over disobedient or contumacious parties (cans. 1743, § 3; 1845, § 1), over advocates and attorneys (cans. 1666; 1663), over those present in the courtroom (can. 1640, § 2), over witnesses (cans. 1766, § 2; 1755, § 3), over experts (can. 1794), and over those who attempt to corrupt the witnesses or experts (can. 1755, § 3).

[19] Cf. Lega-Bartoccetti, *Commentarius in Iudicia Ecclesiastica* (2. ed., 3 vols., Romae: Anonima Libraria Cattolica Italiana, 1950), I, 25.

or juridic: the former being held together purely by ties of mutual friendship and good will without any legal bonds or obligations; the latter, obliging and binding its members with legal effects. Juridic societies may be voluntary or necessary: the former being a creation of man's free will and wish to accomplish a legitimate purpose more easily and more certainly through mutual aid; the latter being imposed upon all men as a necessary means to accomplish an essential purpose of human nature. Necessary societies differ according to the particular potentialities of human nature whose fulfillment is their objective, which may be natural or supernatural, and also according to the origin of the obligation making these societies necessary for the attainment of these essential objectives, which obligation may be founded in either the natural or the positive divine law. Necessary societies are therefore natural or temporal, as the family and the state, or, supernatural or spiritual, as the Church.

Societies are distinguishable again as juridically imperfect and juridically perfect societies: the former being subordinate member societies, which are but a part or means to yet another superior society whose objectives are more basic and complete; the latter being supreme and ultimate in their order, because tending toward the complete, ultimate objective, which in the social order of things are the spiritual and the temporal welfare of mankind.

These juridically perfect societies possess within themselves, at least virtually, all the means necessary for the accomplishment of their purpose, for if the ends to which they tend are obligatory upon men by force of the natural and positive divine law, so too are the means proportionately necessary, and therefore inherent, inalienable rights of the societies, which are themselves necessary means for the accomplishment of these objectives. Juridically perfect societies are, therefore, self-sufficient and independent, and have all the means, actual or virtual, at their command for their proper functioning toward the accomplishment of their purposes.[20]

---

[20] Cf. Ottaviani, *Compendium,* Nos. 8-12; Goldsmith, *The Competence of Church and State over Marriage—Disputed Points,* The Catholic University of America Canon Law Studies, No. 197 (Washington, D. C.: Catholic University of America Press, 1944), p. 17.

Consequently the judicial power of a juridically perfect society comes from outside the human will, having the force and ratification of the law from which it springs, for since judicial power is itself a necessary means for the accomplishment of the ends of any society, it must have the same obligatory force about it as the society itself and the ends which are the object of that society. Hence judicial power is generically defined as a right,[21] or moral faculty,[22] connoting social authority, or the right of obliging members of a society in regard to the accomplishment of its purpose,[23] and as true jurisdiction, i.e., public or sovereign social authority, which is not arbitrarily derived from the will of the members, or from another society, but from the natural and positive divine law.[24]

The judicial power, or authority, of a juridically imperfect society corresponds to the nature of the juridically perfect society of which it is a part, and depends for its existence and measure upon the recognition, delegation, or concession of the juridically perfect society.[25]

The judicial function of the governing agency of a voluntary society, while it may be called an authority, since its decisions are

[21] Cf. *supra*, p. 5

[22] "Ius formaliter sumptum, seu subiective, est moralis seu legitima inviolabilis facultas aliquid faciendi, omittendi aut exigendi."—Coronata, *Ius Publicum Ecclesiasticum*, n. 4.

[23] "Auctoritas . . . est ius obligandi socios in ordine ad finis assecutionem."—*Ibid.*, n. 16.

[24] "Potestas iurisdictionis seu regiminis . . ."—Can. 196. "Iurisdictio est potestas publica regendi subditos in ordine ad finem societatis perfectae consequendum."—Coronata, *Institutiones Iuris Canonici* (2. ed., 5 vols., Taurini: Marietti, 1939-1947), I, n. 275; "potestas iurisdictionis diximus esse potestatem publicam legitimi superioris a Christo, vel ab Ecclesia per canonicam missionem concessam, regendi baptizatos in ordine ad salutem aeternam."—Ottaviani, *Compendium*, n. 71. N.B. That portion of jurisdiction which is possessed within circumscribed limits by a social authority is called competence. "Numerus causarum et diversa earum natura suadent ut iurisdictio inter plures iudices dividatur, certis rationibus limitibus assignatis. Haec iurisdictio limitibus circumscripta competentia appellatur, quae deinde definiri potest; ea pars iurisdictionis, quae unicuique iudici assignatur. Quare competentia a iurisdictione sicut pars a toto differt: et sane quilibet iudex habet iurisdictionem, sed non integram iurisdictionem."—Roberti, *Iuris Processualis Compendium*, I, n. 28.

[25] Coronata, *Ius Publicum Ecclesiasticum*, n. 24.

legally binding, is not true jurisdiction, for its authority is commensurate with the rights willingly ceded to it by the members of the society, and its juridic obligations are chartered, supervised, and enforced by the government of the juridically perfect society under whose domain each particular voluntary society belongs. Hence, the judicial function exercised through the governing agency of a voluntary society is judicial power only in an imperfect sense, and its general social authority is called a dominative power in order that it be properly distinguished from true jurisdictional power.

B. *The Judicial Power of the Church*

> In virtue of their office by the will of God, the Bishops, of whom the Apostle says that they are 'placed by the Holy Ghost to rule the Church of God,' (*Acts,* 20:28), are judges in the Church. 'To rule' includes 'to judge' as a necessary function. Hence according to the Apostle the Holy Spirit calls Bishops to the office of judge no less than to the government of the Church.[26]

Except for those who have been involved in matrimonial cases, most Catholics today are only vaguely aware of the judicial role of their bishops, and of the existence of a judicial system within the Church. This was not always the case. In the Middle Ages the civil and ecclesiastical courts formed a dual system of justice in the everyday life of the people. Oftentimes the political situation was so disrupted by wars and revolution that the Church alone was capable of rendering justice. While the need for such extensive activity is almost non-existent today, and is, indeed, practically impossible, because its God-given authority is so widely unrecognized and rejected today, the judicial system still exists and functions as a proper part of the government of the Church, and as an exclusive authority in purely spiritual matters.[27]

---

[26] Pius XII, Allocution to the Sacred Roman Rota, Oct. 29, 1947—*AAS* XXXIX (1947), 493; Bouscaren, Supplement, p. 218.

[27] Ottaviani notes the unusual circumstances in which the bishops of several cities in Italy assumed the temporal administration of these cities for the common good, when the civil government fled before the advancing allied troops in the years 1944-1945. Cf. *Institutiones Iuris Publici Ecclesiastici,* I, n. 143, footnote n. 100.

Another reason for the layman's unawareness of the judicial power of the Church is that the government of the Church is not separated into branches of divided authority as is our American Republic. All powers and functions of the ecclesiastical government, including the judicial, are held by the Pope,[28] through his divine commission as Vicar of Christ and successor to Saint Peter,[29] and by the bishops, who, by the very fact of their apostolic dignity, are constituted legislator, judge, and executive of their given dioceses.[30]

Nevertheless, the Church does maintain a complete system of courts in order that these authorities may exercise their judicial function effectively. Beginning at the diocesan level, the ordinary of each diocese is required to appoint an *officialis,* or diocesan judge, to conduct the judicial business and to preside in the tribunal of the diocese in the bishop's stead.[31] In this respect the *officialis* in the judicial function of the diocesan government counterbalances the vicar general in the executive, administrative function of the diocesan curia, both forming a legal unity with the ordinary,[32] and both acting with ordinary power in their respective duties.[33] The Code also makes provision for vice-officials,[34] and for all those who are necessary or useful members of a judicial tribunal.[35] Courts of appeal are established on a metropolitan or provincial basis,[36] with final appeal lying to Rome itself.[37] In Rome there is an ordinary tribunal, called the Sacred Roman Rota, to handle the ordinary judicial business of the Holy See, acting as a world court of appeal,[38] and in

---

28 Cans. 1597; 218.

29 Can. 219.

30 Cans. 1572; 335.

31 Can. 1573, § 1.

32 Cans. 1573, § 2; 366; 368.

33 Cans. 1573, § 1; 366, § 1.

34 Can. 1573, § 3.

35 The Code provides for synodal and pro-synodal judges (can. 1574), auditors (can. 1580), notaries (can. 1585), promoters of justice and defenders of the bond (can. 1586), couriers and apparitors (can. 1591), attorneys and advocates (can. 1655), etc.

36 Cans. 1594-6.

37 Can. 1569, § 1.

38 Can. 1598-9.

some cases as a court of first instance,[39] and an extraordinary tribunal of Cardinals, called the Apostolic Signature, which functions as moderator of the Rota.[40]

Moreover, the greater portion of the Fourth Book, ***De Processibus,*** of the Code is given over to judicial matters: courts are recognized and established; the rights and duties of all concerned are stated; competence is regulated; procedures are outlined; norms for the value of proofs, presumptions, and oaths are determined, in order that the Church may justly adjudicate the myriad disputes, quarrels, legal questions, and delicts, which are bound to arise in a world-wide organization charged with the teaching, sanctifying, and regulating of the spiritual life and destiny of men.

The judicial power of the Church falls into the category of the real jurisdiction of a juridically perfect society, for if all men are obliged by the natural and positive divine law to attain to eternal salvation as the supreme and ultimate end of all human life,[41] they are bound to all the means necessary to acquire that end. But since the Church has been made a necessary means for salvation by the positive divine law,[42] and since the judicial power of the Church is a necessary means by which the Church functions, the judicial power receives its obligatory force, or authority, not from the free, contractual consent of the Church's members, nor from the concession of any other society, but from the positive divine law.

Moreover, the rulers of the Church possess judicial power, not only as an integral part of their general authority to rule, but as Matthew has recorded in his Gospel, from the specific commission given by Christ to the Apostles to exercise judicial power. In an instruction delivered to his Apostles,[43] Jesus said:

---

[39] Cans. 1599, § 2; 1557, § 2.

[40] Cans. 1602-5.

[41] "For what does it profit a man, if he gain the whole world, but suffer the loss of his own soul?"—Matthew, 16: 26; "Seek first the kingdom of God and his justice."—Matthew, 6: 33.

[42] "Unless a man be born again of water and the Holy Ghost, he cannot enter into the kingdom of God."—John, 3: 5; "Go into the whole world and preach the gospel to every creature. He who belives and is baptized shall be saved, but he who does not believe shall be condemned."—Mark, 16: 16.

[43] "And at that hour the disciples came to Jesus."—Matthew, 18: 15.

> But if thy brother sin against thee, go and show his fault, between thee and him alone. If he listens to thee, thou hast won thy brother. But if he do not listen to thee, take with thee one or two more, so that on the word of two or three witnesses every word may be confirmed. And if he refuse to hear them, appeal to the Church, but if he refuse to hear even the Church, let him be to thee as the heathen and the publican. Amen I say to you, whatsoever you bind upon earth shall be bound also in heaven; and whatsoever you loose upon earth shall be loosed also in heaven.[44]

In this instruction Jesus made a practical application of His teaching of the love of one's neighbor, which was to extend even to the love of enemies.[45] If Christ knew that scandals must come,[46] He also knew that controversies, disputes, and delicts would rise among Christians. He instructed His Apostles that in this eventuality the injured party shall try to settle the matter first by fraternal correction, and, failing this, by mediation or arbitration. Only as a last resort is there to be "appeal to the Church." [47]

In this event the appeal is no longer a matter of private adjudication. It becomes a matter for public, authoritative settlement, possessing all the elements of real judicial power: the matter is to be settled by the ecclesiastical tribunal pronouncing a definitive and binding sentence (*si autem Ecclesia non audierit: sit tibi sicut ethnicus et publicanus*), arrived at by the process of a judicial trial: the plaintiff making an accusation before a public, ecclesiastical tribunal (*dic Ecclesiae*), that the defendant has committed some crime against him (*peccaverit in te frater tuus*), which is to be proved by witnesses (*unum vel duos, ut in ore duorum, vel trium testium stete omne verbum*).

---

[44] "Si peccaverit in te frater tuus, vade, et corripe eum inter te et ipsum solum; si te audierit, lucratus eris fratrem tuum. Si autem te non audierit, adhibe tecum unum vel duos, ut in ore duorum, vel trium testium stet omne verbum. Quod si non audierit eos, dic Ecclesiae; si autem Ecclesiam non audierit: sit tibi sicut ethnicus et publicanus. Amen dico vobis, quaecumque alligaveritis super terram erunt ligata et in coelo: et quaecumque solveritis super terram erunt soluta et in coelo."—Matthew, 18: 15-18.

[45] Matthew, 5:43-48.

[46] Matthew, 18:7-9.

[47] Matthew, 18:17.

Then Christ addressed the Apostles directly, and in solemn fashion (*Amen dico vobis*) conferred upon them the jurisdiction of performing this spiritual, judicial function of which He had just spoken, promising them the full power of condemning and absolving, and that their sentences are to be ratified in heaven (*quaecumque alligaveritis. . .*).[48] Whence it follows that the judicial power of the Church has its origins in a divine commission. Its authority to judge is, therefore, true jurisdictional power. Its judicial pronouncements are sacred, and both its authority and its pronouncements are independent of the State in origin, character, and purpose.

C. *Principles, and Method to be Followed*

In bestowing this judicial power upon the Church, Christ established a dual judicial system and authority, the one spiritual, the other temporal. But He expressed only the broad outline of their separate functions in His verbal instructions, indicating only that what is Caesar's is to be rendered to Caesar, and what is God's is to be rendered to God.[49]

The key to the intricate and detailed correlation of the two, the principle for determining competence over judicial objects, is the principle of finality.[50] Just as the possession of a proper and exclusive judicial power is itself a corollary of the right of a juridically perfect society to all the means necessary for the attainment of its purposes, so too are the objects of that judicial power to be determined by their relationship as means, or as impediments, to the ends of the society.

Objects may fall within the jurisdiction of a society either properly or accidentally, exclusively or cumulatively. Those belong properly which naturally affect the society, receiving their finality from their intrinsic nature, from the positive disposition of the divine will, or

---

[48] This interpretation of this text is apparently part of the ordinary *magisterium* of the Church. Cf., especially, Ottaviani, *Compendium,* n. 85; also, Bender, *Ius Publicum Ecclesiasticum* (Bussum in Hollandia: Paulus Brand, 1948), p. 79; Marchesi, *Summula Iuris Publici Ecclesiastici* (Neapoli: M. d'Auria, 1948), n. 63.

[49] Matthew, 22:21-22.

[50] Cf. Leo XIII, ep. encycl., *Immortale Dei—Fontes,* n. 592, *The Catholic Mind,* Nov. 8, 1936, pp. 431-2.

from the disposition of the Church adapting a natural object to supernatural purposes.[51] Those belong accidentally which receive an indirect finality towards a society by reason of human concession, agreement, or exceptional circumstances, as matters of concordat and devolved power. Those belong exclusively to the jurisdiction of a society which affect that society alone. Those belong cumulatively to the jurisdiction of both societies which affect both societies indisciminately.

Since there is no superior with whom appeal can be lodged when the Church and State become involved in controversy as to their relative competence, the decision is to be made by the Church. This right of the Church depends first on its gift of teaching infallibly concerning faith and morals, so that it cannot err concerning the determination of its own mission and authority. It depends secondly on its indirect superiority to the State, for the peace and material prosperity of this present life, which is the object of the judicial power of the State, is not the end-all and the be-all of life, but rather the means by which man may more securely, and more readily, gain eternal life.[52]

Knowledge of the divine plan concerning the functioning of the judicial power of the Church, as it emerges from its implicit status in the teachings of Christ, is to be gained, therefore, from a study of history and of the practice and legislation of the Church concerning this point. History provides an unerring guide in so far as the constant practice of the Church, the unanimous teachings of its doctors, and the decrees of pontiffs and councils in the face of persecution and establishment, of faith and secularism, form that body of ordi-

---

[51] "Ultimo ex dictis intelligitur posse aliquando Pontificem determinare materiam aliquam seu quasi reservare illam, ut tantum canonica sit, non solum declarando, ut sine dubio facere potest, quando materia ipsa ex se et ex iure divino spiritualis est, sed etiam constituendo et eximendo sibique reservando aliquam materiam propter spiritualem rationem, etiam si alias secundum se posset esse materia legum civilium."—Suarez, *De Legibus,* Cap. XI, n. 2. (*Selections from Three Works of Francisco Suarez,* Carnegie Endowment for International Peace, 2 vols.: photographic reproduction and English translation [New York: The Oxford Press, Oxford: The Clarendon Press, 1944] [hereafter cited *Selections*]).

[52] Wernz-Vidal, *Ius Canonicum ad Codicis Normam Exactum* (7 vols. in 9, Romae: apud Aedes Universitatis Gregorianae, 1923-1938), VI, n. 20.

nary teaching and general discipline which are the norms for the orderly and salutary conduct of men as individuals and as societies. The legislation of the Church in the present day is the fruit of these tradition-laden centuries, crystalizing the teachings of the Church, and authoritatively enunciating the principles for the determination of its proper and exclusive jurisdiction by right of its divine mission.[53]

---

[53] Cf. Bouix, *Tractatus De Iudiciis Ecclesiasticis,* I, 67-72.

PART I—HISTORY OF THE JUDICIAL POWER OF THE CHURCH

Chapter II

THE ROMAN ERA

A. *The Apostolic Period*

The Apostles understood that they had been given the power to judge with divine authority when Christ told them, "Whatsoever you bind upon earth shall be bound also in heaven." [1] Such a divinely ratified power was demonstratively exercised by Peter when he condemned Ananias and Sapphira of fraud in keeping back part of the price of the land they had promised to contribute to the Church. Both were stricken dead at the feet of their judge.[2] Again St. Paul judged the incestuous Corinthian,[3] and also Hymeneus and Alexander, because they had "made shipwreck of the Faith." [4] Further, the Apostles gave counsels and instructions concerning the exercise of this power by the Church. Thus St. Paul counselled the Corinthians to appoint Christians as judges even in "cases about worldly matters," [5] and admonished Timothy not to listen to an accusation against a presbyter, "unless it is supported by two or three witnesses." [6] The Apostles, therefore, recognized and exercised a judicial power in regard to faith, morals, and discipline.

In the light of Christ's statement before Pilate, "My kingdom is not of this world," [7] Saint Paul gave an unexpected determination to the limits of the judicial power of the Church when he said:

> Dare any of you, having a matter against another, bring your case to be judged before the unjust and not before the saints? Do you not know that the saints will judge the world? And if the world will be judged by you, are you unworthy to judge

---

1 Matthew, 18:18.

2 *Acts of the Apostles,* 5:5 and 10.

3 *I Corinthians,* 5:3-5.

4 *I Timothy,* 1:20.

5 *I Corinthians,* 6:1-14.

6 *I Timothy,* 5:19.

7 John, 18:31.

> the smallest matters? Do you not know that we shall judge angels? How much more worldly things! If, therefore, you have cases about worldly matters to be judged, appoint those who are rated as nothing in the Church to judge. To shame you I say it. Can it be that there is not one wise man among you competent to settle a case in his brother's matter? But brother goes to law with brother and that before unbelievers.[8]

It cannot be believed that Paul wished either to usurp temporal power, or to deny the rightful authority of the State in temporal affairs, but he did deplore the existence of such controversies and arguments among Christians, and the fact that Christians were not governed entirely by supernatural charity, which "bears with all things. . . endures all things," as he taught in a later chapter of this same letter.[9] Far from seeking to destroy the authority of civil rulers in temporal matters, Paul and the Apostles often urged the faithful to be obedient to their princes and rulers, for "there exists no authority except from God, and those who exist have been appointed by God. Therefore he who resists authority resists God,"[10] and yet Paul acknowledged that the Church has jurisdiction to settle the temporal affairs of the faithful, for he not only counselled and admonished, but gave a precept that the faithful should submit their disputes concerning worldly affairs to the Church, as is implied by his terminology, "Dare any of you!"[11]

This right, however, was not necessarily universal and absolute; it can be interpreted to mean that Christians could not submit their disputes to secular courts during that particular time for reasons of scandal, or in view of the danger of apostacy in consequence of the demand to swear by false gods, etc. This Pauline doctrine, then, need not imply a direct judicial power over temporal matters on the part of the Church, but only an indirect one, in so far as this activity was demanded by the spiritual welfare of society, as for the protection of consciences and of Christian morals when these were endangered, or could not be preserved by the ordinary temporal process.[12]

---

[8] *I Corinthians,* 6:1-6.

[9] *Ibid.,* 13:4-7.

[10] *Romans,* 13:1-2; cf. also *Titus,* 3:1; *I Peter,* 2:13-17.

[11] Cf. Ottaviani, *Institutiones Iuris Publici Ecclesiastici,* II, n. 161.

[12] Ottaviani *loc. cit.*

Only one restriction was placed upon this power by St. Paul. In condemning the incestuous Corinthian he stated, "I wrote to you in the letter not to associate with the immoral—not meaning, of course, the immoral of this world. . . . For what do I have to do with judging those outside? Is it not those inside whom you judge? For those outside God will judge." [13] Thus the judicial jurisdiction of the Church is limited, according to St. Paul, to those "inside" the Church, i.e., the baptized.

The relationship of the Church with the civil courts became evident shortly after the crucifixion, when the infant Church again found itself before the court of the Sanhedrin. When ordered to cease and desist from its teaching and preaching, the Apostles boldly proclaimed, "Whether it is right in the sight of God to listen to you rather than to God, decide for yourselves. For we cannot but speak of what we have seen and heard," [14] and, upon the occasion of their second arrest and trial, "We must obey God rather than men." [15]

The Apostles, then, applying and interpreting the teachings and actions of their Master, proclaimed their mission to be divine, and as such absolutely independent of any human jurisdiction, even that of the Jewish Law. This they maintained by disregarding the two injunctions of the Sanhedrin, by accepting the scourges and persecutions which they received for this contempt, and by continuing their mission so that, "They did not for a single day cease teaching and preaching from house to house the good news of Jesus as the Christ." [16]

It was not long before the dispute was brought into the Roman courts. On each occasion, as in the trial of Christ Himself, the court was asked to take jurisdiction on the grounds of public disorder.[17] In Macedonia, for instance, the charge was, "These men

---

[13] *I Corinthians*, 5:9-13.

[14] *Acts of the Apostles*, 4:9-20.

[15] *Ibid.*, 5:29-30.

[16] *Ibid.*, 5:42.

[17] "And the whole assemblage rose, and took him before Pilate. And they began to accuse him saying, 'We have found this man perverting our nation, and forbidding the payment of taxes to Caesar, and saying that he is Christ a king . . . . He is stirring up the people.' "—Luke, 23:1-5.

are making a great disturbance in our city,"[18] while in Jerusalem the Romans wrenched Paul from the hands of a murderous mob and placed him under protective custody. In this case, when the high priest Ananias appeared five days later to make formal charges, he asserted, "We found this man a pest, a promoter of seditions among all the Jews throughout the world, and a ringleader of the sedition of the Nazarene sect. He even tried to desecrate the temple, but we caught him and wished to judge him according to our Law."[19] Thus the formal charge was disturbance of the peace, with the religious issue offered as an explanatory background. From this it appears that the Roman judges refused to concern themselves with the purely religious matters of the Jewish Law, just as Pilate had wished to do when he understood that the charges against Jesus were purely of a religious nature.[20]

This was confirmed by an event in Achaia where there occurred the only case, as related in the *Acts of the Apostles,* in which the Jews charged Paul upon strictly religious grounds.[21] Here Gallio the proconsul ruled, "If there were some question of misdemeanor or serious crime, O Jews, I should with reason bear with you. But if these are questions of word and of names and of your Law, look to it yourselves; I have no wish to decide such matters."[22] Thus even under the Roman Protectorate of Palestine the civil courts operated on the political policy that religious squabbles of its subjects concerning belief or discipline were of no concern to the State, but were subject to the authority of the religious societies themselves.[23]

---

18 *Acts of the Apostles,* 16:20.

19 *Ibid.,* 21:27-36; 24:1-9.

20 John 18:28-40.

21 "This fellow is persuading men to worship God contrary to the Law."—*Acts,* 18:12-17. The text here quoted is found in verse 13.

22 *Ibid.,* verses 14-15.

23 The same policy was set out, though in a somewhat different historical context, in a law of Emperors Arcadius (395-408), and Honorius (395-423) in the year 398. It is interpreted in the *Theodosian Code* in the following manner: "Iudaei omnes, qui Romani esse noscuntur, hos solum apud religionis suae maiores agunt, quod ad religionis eorum pertinet disciplinam, ita ut inter se, quae sunt Hebraeis legibus statuta custodiant. Alia uero negotia, quae nostris legibus continentur et ad forum respiciunt, apud iudicem prouinciae eo quo omnes iure confligant . . . consentientes ambae

This policy was not, of course, based on a respect for divine authority in spiritual matters. It was simply a matter of expediency. The Romans did not wish to incur the wrath of any segment of their subjugated populace by taking sides in their wrangling, which was of no interest or profit to the Roman State. They had no scruples about interfering in their own established State religion.

It is to be noted that Paul, as a Roman citizen, often sought the protection of the civil authority. In Macedonia he threatened to bring action against the officials who beat him without previous benefit of a trial though he was a Roman citizen,[24] and in Jerusalem he refused to give himself up to the Sanhedrin, appealing instead to Caesar.[25] The protective role of the State was to be developed in later centuries, and the Christians would refer to the actions of Paul as authoritative precedents to justify their use of the civil authority to protect the Church and themselves.[26]

Thus in the Apostolic period the Church exercised a divinely ratified judicial power. This power extended beyond matters of faith, morals, and discipline, to the settlement of temporal disputes among Christians. It was limited to the baptized. The Church denied any judicial rights on the part of the State, or of the Sanhedrin, to interfere with its divine mission. The policy of the Roman State was one of non-interference in spiritual or religious disputes, except when they involved some "misdemeanor or serious crime," and thus affected the public order and welfare of the State and its citizens. The Apostles sometimes sought the protection of the civil courts.

B. *The Persecutions*

The Church continued to demonstrate its independent and absolute character by its steadfastness under persecution. The Emperors could torture and kill the individual Christians, but the Church grew from the seed of martyrs. Indeed, the very hostility of the State prevented

---

partes, de solo tamen ciuili negotio . . . compromisso arbitrali iudicio terminatur. . . ."—*Codex Theodosianus* (ed. Krueger, Berolini: apud Weidmannos, 1923-1926), (2, 1), 10, *Interpretatio* (hereinafter cited: *C. Th.*).

[24] *Acts of the Apostles*, 16:35-40.

[25] *Ibid.*, 21-26.

[26] Cf., for example, c. 7, D. X.

it from intervening in, influencing, or licensing the activities of the Church, so that the latter appeared as the ultimate and supreme authority. The State's attitude served to accentuate and emphasize the proper and exclusive power of the Church in spiritual and ecclesiastical matters.

It cannot be objected that during this period the Church exercised its judicial powers only in the internal forum of conscience. While the form of judicial procedure was admittedly in its embryonic stage, the matters treated were grave and public, and often involved recalcitrants who were certainly not motivated by penance. Pope Anicetus (155-166), for example, in the year 160 settled the bitter dispute over the date upon which Easter was to be celebrated,[27] and Pope Victor I (189-199) excommunicated all Asiatics who refused to accept this decision.[28] Judicial procedure evinced a development during this period. For example, St. Cyprian (258) in a letter to Pope Cornelius (251-253) concerning the *lapsi* expounded the principle that the competency of an episcopal tribunal was to be determined from the location of the crime.[29] Thus even during the persecutions, the Church exercised judicial power in the external forum, independently of the State.

Inasmuch as the Church had no standing with the State, the scope of its decisions was necessarily limited to purely spiritual matters. If temporal matters were submitted to the Church for adjudication, it was on a strictly voluntary basis of arbitration, for its decisions carried no weight before the civil court. To enforce its pronouncements the Church could employ only moral persuasion and ecclesiastical penalties. Though its courts were unrecognized, the Church, in the midst of persecution, enjoyed an unlimited freedom of action in its

---

[27] Cf. Eusebius, *Historia Ecclesiastica,* V, 23-25 (Migne, *Patrologiae Cursus Completus, Series Graeca,* 161 vols., Parisiis, 1857-1866, XX, cols. 499-503 (hereafter cited *MPG*).

[28] Cf. Eusebius, *Historia Ecclesiastica,* V, 24 (*MPG,* XX, col. 498), Jaffé, *Regesta Pontificum Romanorum ab condita Ecclesiae ad annum post Christum natum MCXCVIII* (2 ed., correctam et auctam auspiciis Gulielmi Wattenbach, curaverunt S. Löwenfeld, F. Kaltenbrunner, P. Ewald, 2 vols., Lipsiae, 1885-1888), n. 73.

[29] *Ep. XII ad Cornelium* (Migne, *Patrologiae Cursus Completus, Series Latina,* 221 vols. Parisiis, 1844-1855), III, cols. 821-2 (hereafter cited *MPL*).

internal affairs, which it was later partially to sacrifice as the price of becoming the official religion of the Roman State.[30]

C. *Emperor Constantine I* (*306-337*)

Though the Emperor Constantine has proved to be a most controversial figure in history, it is certain that with the restoration of peace by Constantine in 313, the authority and nature of ecclesiastical judicial power were recognized for the first time. Indeed Constantine himself declared:

> God has constituted you priests, and He has given you power to judge even us. Rightly, therefore, are we judged by you, but you cannot be judged by men. For this reason you must await the judgment of God alone upon you; and your disputes, whatever they may be, are to be reserved for the scrutiny of the Divinity. For you have been given to us as gods, and it is not fitting that men should judge gods, but only He, of whom it is written, 'God stood in the synagogue of the gods, in their midst does God judge.'[31]

This statement, made by Constantine at the Council of Nicaea (325), was a declaration of his policy with regard to the basic principles which were to govern the judicial relationship of Church and State. As drawn from the text they are: 1) civil recognition of the judicial power of the Church (*Deus . . . potestatem vobis dedit, de nobis quoque judicandi*); 2) the exclusive jurisdiction of the Church in spiritual matters (*vestra jurgia quaecumque sunt ad illud divinum reservantur examen*); 3) the immunity of spiritual persons from the jurisdiction of civil courts (*vos autem non potestis ab*

---

[30] Cf. Alzog, *Manual of Universal Church History* (translated by Pabisch and Byrne in 3 vols., Cincinnati, Ohio, 1874), I, 646; Cappello, *Summa Iuris Publici Ecclesiastici* (2. ed., Romae: apud Aedes Universitatis Gregorianae, 1928), n. 297.

[31] "Deus vos constituit sacerdotes et potestatem vobis dedit de nobis quoque judicandi, et ideo nos a vobis recte judicamur, vos autem non potestis ab hominibus judicari. Propter quod Dei solius inter vos expectate judicium, et vestra jurgia quaecumque sunt, ad illud divinum reservantur examen. Vos etenim nobis a Deo dati estis dii, et conveniens non est ut homo judicet deos, sed ille solus de quo scriptum est: Deus stetit in synagoga deorum, in medio autem deus judicat (Ps. 81)."—Rufinus, *Historia Ecclesiastica,* I, 2 (*MPL,* XXI, col. 468).

hominibus judicari), and 4) the superiority of the authority of the Church (*nos a vobis recte judicabimur*).

Civil recognition of the judicial power of the Church implied that the decisions of the Church courts were to be considered as legally binding upon Catholics before the civil law, and whereas during the persecutions the Church had been able to enforce its judicial sentences only by way of moral compulsion and spiritual penalties, now the State was ready to lend the supplementary support of temporal penalties, as did Constantine in both the Donatist and the Arian heresies.[32]

---

[32] His rescript at the close of the Council of Arles (314) reads: "Redite ad proprias sedes; meique mementote, ut mei salvator noster semper misereatur. Ceterum direxi meos homines, qui eosdem infandos deceptores religionis protinus ad comitatum meum perducant, ut ibi degant, ibi sibi mortem pervideant. Dedi quoque litteras competentes ad eum, qui vicariam praefecturam per Africam tuetur, ut quotquot huius insanae similes invenerit, statim eos ad comitatum meum diregat, ne ulterius sub tanta claritate Dei nostri ea ab ipsis fiant, quae maximam iracundiam coelestis providentiae possint incitare. Incolumus vos Deus omnipotens, tribuat votis meis et vestris per saecula, fratres carissimi."—*Ex Appendice ad Optatum* (Mansi, *Sacrorum Conciliorum Nova et Amplissima Collectio*, 53 vols in 60 Parisiis, Arnhem, Leipzig, 1901-1927), II, col. 478 (hereafter cited Mansi). The appendix of Optatus is thought to be a seventh book added by him on the occasion of his revision of his work, but published only posthumously, and not too faithfully by another. Cf. E. Amann, "Optat de Milève, Saint,"—*Dictionnaire de Théologie Catholique*, 15 vols. in 30, with the *Tables Generales* (Paris: Libraire Letouzey et Ané, 1903-1951), XIII, cols. 1077-84.

At the close of the I Council of Nicaea (325), Constantine ordered: "Cum malignos et impios Arius sibi imitandos duxerit, par est, ut eamdem cum illis ferat ignominiam. . . . Si quod autem scriptum ab Ario compositum reperiatur, igni tradatur, ut non modo improba ejus doctrina tollatur, verum etiam ne monumentum quidem aliquod ejus relinquatur. Illud equidem praedictum volo, si quis libellum aliquem ab Ario conscriptum occultasse deprehensis sit, ne continuo eum prolatum igne absumpserit, morte mulctabitur. Illico namque in crimine tali comprehensus poenam capitis luet."—*Gelasii Cyzicensis Commentarius*, II, 36 (Mansi, II, col. 919). This work of Gelasius is a compilation of Eusebius, Rufinus, Theodoret, and other sources to which Gelasius had almost exclusive access. The research of M. Loeschke, *Das Syntagma des Gelasius Cyzicenus* (Bonn, 1906), has restored Gelasius to his rightful place among the serious historians of the Church. Cf. P. Godet, "Gélase," *Dictionnaire de Théologie Catholique*, VI, cols. 1182-3; also, Edward Myers, "Gelasius of Cyzicus," *Catholic*

Constantine did not consider such actions to be in conflict with his policy of non-interference in spiritual matters. His expressed intention was to supplement the power of the Church when its bishops were unable to preserve the unity and well-being of the Church. Indeed, he appeared very indignant when the heretics carried their appeal to his civil authority.[33] His summoning of the Council of Rome (313) to hear this case was excused by Optatus on the grounds that Constantine was, *"adhuc in fide rudis et formam ecclesiasticorum ignorat,"* and because he ordered nothing to be defined without the knowledge, consent, and authority of the Roman Pontiff.[34] It was in this role of protector of the external welfare of the Church that Constantine styled himself as "an external bishop" of the Church,[35] and though he retained his title as *Pontifex Maximus,* he did so, it is asserted, to strengthen his authority and political power among the pagans.[36]

The exemption of clerics and religious from the jurisdiction of the civil courts has its origin even at this early date in the history of the Church. So great was Constantine's proposed respect for the clergy, and so searching seemed to be his understanding of the scandal that could arise from the publication of their faults, that Constantine declared that he would turn his eyes away if he saw a cleric committing a sin.[37]

Encyclopedia (15 vols., Index and 2 Supplements, New York, 1907-1922), VI, 407.

[33] Having read the *libellus* appealing the case of the Donatists, "Constantinus pleno livore respondit. In qua responsione et eorum preces prodidit, dum ait, 'Petitis a me in seculo judicem, cum ego ipse Christi judicium expectem."—*Synodus Romana Miltiadis ex Optati Libro* I (Mansi, II, col. 436); and again, "O rabida furoris audicia, sicut in causis Gentilium fieri solet, appelationem interposuerunt."—*ibid.,* cols. 437, 478.

[34] *Ibid.,* cols. 434-5; Consult, however, Coleman, *Constantine the Great and Christianity* (New York: the Columbia University Press, 1914), pp. 61-71, concerning the motive and activity of Constantine in Church affairs.

[35] "Quocirca non absurde, cum episcopos aliquando convivio exciperet, se quoque episcopum esse dixerit, hic fere verbis usus nobis presentibus, 'Vos, quidem, inquit, in iis quae intra Ecclesiam sunt, episcopi estis. Ego vero in iis quae extra gerantur episcopus a Deo sum constitutus'."—Eusebius, *Vita Constantini,* IV, 24 (*MPG,* II, cols. 953-4).

[36] Alzog, *Manual of Universal Church History,* I, 468-70.

[37] "[Constantinus] ajebat enim sacerdotum delicta vulgo ignota esse

Constantine explicitly acknowledged that even the Emperor fell within the jurisdiction of the judicial power of the Church. Further, his estimation of the Church and of bishops was such that he allowed the Christians to submit even their temporal disputes to Christian judges.[38] For this purpose he delegated to bishops the right of giving definitive sentences in cases in which the litigating parties were dissatisfied with the decisions of the secular judges.[39]

In the present connection a word should be said about the so-called "Donation of Constantine." In this text, which is incorporated in the *Decretum of Gratian*,[40] but which is wholly spurious,[41] Constantine purportedly granted many privileges to the Pope and the Roman clergy, such as ecclesiastical supremacy over the entire Church, the office of judge in questions of faith and worship, as well as temporal sovereignty over Rome and Italy. Historians have used this text for the purpose of explaining and also for the purpose of explaining away the powers of the Papacy. The Pontiffs of the Middle Ages, accepting the document at its face value, used it as a means of bolstering their claims of jurisdiction, which rested primarily and solidly on

---

opertere, ne inde scandali occasione arrepta, minore cum metu delinquant. Ferunt ipsum et hoc etiam addidisse, quod si quando ipse suis oculis viderit episcopum alienae uxori stuprum inferentem, si tua purpura flagitium contecturum, ne intuentium oculi facinore ipso offenderentur. Tanta erat imperatoris et tam pia atque admirabilis prudentia."—*Gelasii Cyzicensis Commentarius Actorum Concilii Nicaeni* (Mansi, II, col. 819); cf. *supra*, footnote no. 32, p. 28.

[38] This was in conformity with the Pauline doctrine that the Church possessed such power. *I Corinthians*, 6:1-14; cf. *supra*, pp. 21-2.

[39] Such a law attributed to Constantine is found in the *Theodosian Code*: "Iudex pro sua sollicitudine obseruare debebit, ut, si ad episcopale iudicium prouocetur, silentium accommodet et, si quis ad legem Christianum negotium transferre uoluerit et illud iudicium obseruare, audiatur, etiamsi negotium apud iudicem sit inchoatum, et pro sanctis habetur, quidquid ab his fuerit iudicatum: ita tamen, ne usurpetur in eo, ut unus ex litigantibus pergat ad supra dictum auditorium et arbitrium suum enuntiet. Judex enim, praesentis causae integro haberi debet arbitrium, ut omnibus accepto latis pronuntiet." —*C. Th.* (1, 27), 1 (318).

[40] C. 14, D. CXVI.

[41] Cf. Hergenröther, *Catholic Church and Christian State* (2 vols. in 1, London, 1876), Essay XII, Part II, Vol. 2, pp. 164-72; and Coleman, *Constantine the Great and Christianity*, Part III, pp. 175-209.

a theological basis, with this confirmation from human authority, though at a later time Protestants claimed to find in it an explanation that the powers of the Pope rested on medieval politics and ideas, such as this mistaken acceptance of a forged document which purports to cede authority from a purely human source. It is to be noted, however, that the use of this document as an argument for the power of the Popes was always considered as secondary and simply corroborative in nature. There always dominated the concept that papal authority was given by divine commission, and not by a human emperor.[42]

With Constantine, then, and the return of peace, the judicial power of the Church, its independent character (though sometimes interfered with in practice by an Emperor whose motives have been questioned and challenged by historians), its exclusive and proper jurisdiction over spiritual matters, its superiority to civil authority, and its function in regard to temporal affairs, were recognized, and its decisions upheld by the State.

D. *The Theodosian and Justinian Codes*

Constantine could not entirely eradicate from the Roman mentality the old idea that the Church was subject to the State. Accordingly his successors fostered and protected the Church according to their various whims and individual dispositions. It is curious to note that the Church enjoyed a greater freedom in its judicial activities under Constantine, whose motives were suspect, than under the Christian emperors who succeeded him.[43]

The existence of ecclesiastical courts as an integral part of the judicial system was never challenged, and the right of appeal from the secular courts to the bishops, though varying in the limits of the required conditions, was carried down through the Middle Ages.[44]

---

[42] Cf. Hergenröther, *loc. cit.*; Ullmann, *Medieval Papalism,* (London: Methuen & Co., 1949); *infra,* footnote no. 5, pp. 39-40.

[43] Cf. Boyd, *The Ecclesiastical Edicts of the Theodosian Code,* Faculty of Political Science, Columbia University (New York, 1905), pp. 21-32; 38-54.

[44] The right of a plaintiff or defendant to appeal to the bishop in a civil trial, even against the objections of his opponent, is found (but not maintained, cf. c. 7, X, *de appelatione,* II, XXVIII) in the *Decretals* of Gregory IX, *de iudiciis,* quoting the famous letter *Novit* of Innocent III, who claimed that

The civil courts, hindered by unwieldy processes and undue delays, were so often passed over by litigants in favor of Church courts, that the boundaries of ecclesiastical jurisdiction were sometimes bitterly contested.[45] Typical of the resultant major restrictions placed upon episcopal courts by the Emperors as found in the *Code of Theodosius* (438) and the *Code* and *Novels of Justinian* (529 and 534),[46] are these:

In June, 376, the Emperor Gratian (375-383) ruled that certain dissensions and minor delicts pertaining to the observance of religion were to be heard by the diocesan synod.[47]

In 398 Arcadius (395-408) and Honorius (395-423) demanded that the appeal to the bishop be voluntary on the part of both parties, but allowed no appeal from the decision of the bishop.[48]

In the same year Honorius further restricted contentious causes

---

this edict of Theodosius had been confirmed by Charlemagne. The edict reads as follows: "Quicunque vidilicet litem habens, sive petitor fuerit sive reus, sive in initio litis vel decursis temporum curriculis, sive quum negotium peroratur, sive quum iam coeperit promi sententia, si iudicium elegerit sacrosanctae sedis antitistis, illico sine aliqua dubitatione, etiamsi pars alia refragetur, ad episcoporum judicium cum sermone litigantium dirigatur."—c. 13, X, *de judiciis*, II, 1.

[45] Cf. Boyd, *The Ecclesiastical Edicts of the Theodosian Code*, pp. 101-2.

[46] *Codex Iustinianus* (ed. P. Krueger, ed. stereotypa decima, Berolini: apud Weidmannos, 1929) (hereafter cited *C. Iust.*); *Novellae* (edd. R. Schoell et G. Kroll, ed. stereotypa quinta Berolini: apud Weidmannos, 1928).

[47] "Qui mos est causarum civilium, idem in negotiis ecclesiasticis obtinendus est: ut, si qua sunt ex quibusdam dissensionibus levibusque delictis ad religionis observantiam pertinentia, locis suis et a suae dioeceseos synodis audiantur: exceptis quae actio criminalis ab ordinariis extraordinariisque iudicibus aut inlustribus potestatibus audienda constituit."—*C. Th.* (16, 2) 23.

[48] "Episcopale iudicium sit ratum omnibus, qui se audiri a sacerdotibus elegerint, eamque illorum iudicationi adhibendam esse reverentiam quam vestris referre necesse est potestatibus, a quibus non licet provocare. Per iudicum quoque officia, ne sit cassa episcopalis cognitio, definitioni executio tribuatur."—*C. Iust.* (1, 4) 8; "Si quis ex consensu apud sacrae legis antistitem litigare uoluerint, non uetabuntur, sed experientur illius (in ciuili dumtaxat negotio) arbitri more residentis sponte iudicium. Quod his obesse non potuerit nec debebit, quos ad praedicti cognitoris examen conuentos potius afuisse quam sponte uenisse constiterit."—*C. Th.* (1, 27) 2; *C. Iust.* (1, 4) 7.

to those which involved religious questions. All others were to be tried by the Roman courts.[49]

In the year 539 Justinian I (527-565) enacted two laws which provide an insight into the nature of the episcopal courts of the time. A law of April of that year demanded that if anyone had any type of suit against a monk or a religious, it was to be settled by the proper bishop, who was to judge the case in an honest and priestly manner, and according to both the civil and ecclesiastical laws. This was to be done in order that the question might be definitely settled without the dragging of it through the double process of the civil and the ecclesiastical courts, so that the minds of the religious might not be preoccupied with legal troubles, but might swiftly be freed for their sacred work.[50]

In August of the same year, another law was passed concerning the *privilegium fori,* in which any suits involving the financial affairs of clerics were to be tried first by the proper bishop. His decision was to be final (and thus there was eliminated all contest in the civil courts), but only if the parties so wished and requested. If, however, the nature or the difficulty of the case made it impossible for the bishop to decide the matter, then the civil judges were to settle it. If the case was of a criminal nature, it was to be tried by the competent civil judge, and if the accused was found guilty and worthy of punishment, he was first to be deposed by the bishop, in order thus to be brought under subjection to the civil law. The *Novella* added that if there was question of an ecclesiastical delict that called for an ecclesiastical penalty, the bishop was to hear the case to the exclusion of civil judges, since these were to proceed according to the sacred and divine rules which the civil laws respectfully reverenced.[51]

Such cases, then, with either laymen or religious involved, were subject to the bishop, the right of appeal to the civil authority being honored, however, unless it was waived by both parties. Only delicts

---

49 "Quotiens de religione agitur, episcopos convenit agitare; certeras vero causas, quae ad ordinarios cognitores vel ad usum publici iuris pertinent, legibus oportet audiri."—*C. Th.* (16, 11) 1.

50 *Novellae,* 79, 1-2.

51 *Novellae,* 84 (83 in *Authenticum*), 1-2.

of a strictly ecclesiastical nature were recognized as falling exclusively under the bishop's jurisdiction.

The secular power of this age exercised a directive and controlling power over the ecclesiastical judiciary. Justinian's *Novellae,* for instance, required that each archbishop and patriarch should convene his suffragan bishops once or twice a year for the purpose of carefully examining and settling any disputes which the clergy might have among themselves.[52] The very next *caput* (11) forbids bishops and priests from excommunicating anyone before showing legal cause, and also forbids bishops from striking anyone. *Caput* twenty of the same *Novella* establishes penalties for any priests or deacons who commit perjury. Besides determining the scope of episcopal arbitration, and supervising the espiscopal courts, the civil courts themselves heard cases of heresy,[53] which was a civil as well as an ecclesiastical offense.[54]

Correlative to all this supervision on the part of the State was the extension of the Church's surveillance into temporal fields. Besides calling for their arbitration in temporal cases, the civil law required that the bishops visit the jails every week to inquire into the crimes committed to ascertain the treatment given the prisoners, and to submit a report of their findings to the government.[55] The Church also championed the cause of the unfortunates to the extent that it was considered one of the duties of priests to snatch the condemned from death whenever this could be done without disturbance. [56]

[52] *Novellae,* 123 (*Authenticum,* 134), 10.

[53] Boyd, who devoted a whole chapter of his study of the *Theodosian Code* to this particular function of the courts, held that this work was carried out by the ordinary civil courts. He could find only one instance which provided for a special civil tribunal for this work. *C. Th.* (16, 5) 9.

[54] Indeed, the very first title of *Justinian's Code* is concerned *De Summa Trinitate, et de Fide Catholica, et ut Nemo de Ea Publice Contendere Audeat,* while Theodosius devoted the entire sixteenth book of his Code to ecclesiastical matters. The following may serve as examples: "In haereticis erroribus quoscumque constiterit vel ordinasse clericos vel suscepisse officium clericorum, denis libris auri viritim mulctandos esse censemus."—Valentinian II (392), (16, 5) 21; ". . . omnes clerici haereticorum ex sacratissima urbe pellantur, neque his finibus liceat convenire."—*Ibid.,* 30.

[55] *C. Iust.* (1, 4) 22.

[56] Instruction of St. Ambrose, Bishop of Milan, *De Officiis,* II, 29—*MPL,* XVI, cols. 142-4.

The Church engaged in such work, not from the wish to usurp the functions of the State, but solely from a consciousness of its duty to promote justice and to practice charity, as is evident from the complaints of the spiritual-minded clergy of the time. Chrysostom (354-407), for example, complained: "The difficulties of clerical arbitration are greater than those of the public judge, for it is hard for him to find the law, and once having found it, difficult also not to violate it,"[57] while St. Augustine (354-430) observed that people voluntarily seek the arbitration of the bishop, but are discontent when they cannot appeal a case which was decided against them.[58]

The latter days of the Roman Empire can be characterized thus: From the time of Constantine, when the existence of Christianity was formally recognized, and the Church acknowledged as an institution to be protected and venerated by the State, its disciplinary laws were no longer found solely in ecclesiastical canons and decrees, nor were its punishments solely of a spiritual character and intended only by persons who gave voluntary submission. The several codes of the Empire considered its subjects to be Christian, and frequently adopted and sanctioned laws enacted originally as purely ecclesiastical legislation by either incorporating such laws into the civil code, or by granting the ecclesiastical authority the power to call in the secular arms to enforce its decisions. This change in the relations of Church and State gave a civil aspect to many spiritual delicts, for which the application of punishment still remained within the competence of the Church. Discipline was thenceforward enforced partly by the spiritual, partly by the temporal, arm. The vigor of the reinforcement of the State varied acording to the disposition of the rulers at the time. The ecclesiastical authorities made constant efforts to withdraw the clergy from the jurisdiction of the civil courts altogether.[59]

---

57 *De Sacredotio,* III, 17 (*MPL,* XLVIII, col. 658).

58 *Commentary on the Psalms,* XXV, 13 (*MPL,* XXXVI, cols. 195-6).

59 Cf. Cappello, *Summa Iuris Publici Ecclesiastici,* nos. 277-8; Walter G. P. Phillimore, "Discipline," *A Dictionary of Christian Antiquities* (2 vols., ed. by Sir Wm. Smith, Hartford, 1880), I, 566-8.

Chapter III

THE AGES OF CHRISTENDOM

A. *The Relationship of Church and State during the Ages of Christendom*

When the Church crossed the Alps to christianize and civilize Europe, its position was quite the reverse of what it had held under the Roman Empire. No longer was there a strong secular power ready to patronize the Church with its temporal might, but rather there was a group of embryonic nations, whose leaders saw in the Church the erudition, the moral coercion, the unifying allegiance, which could be used as tools for political ambitions. Consequently the kings espoused the cause of the Church, and the nobles sought positions of ecclesiastical authority which carried with them political influence and temporal wealth.[1]

The interlacing of Church and State became further complicated through the crowning of Charlemagne as Emperor of all Christendom by Leo III in the year 800. Oftentimes the youthful secular powers ruled with unbridled tyranny, or plagued by internal revolts, were unwilling, or unable, to render justice. The medieval popes, caught in such an era of political upheaval with its Crusades and newly emerging civilization, intervened in feudal disputes, settled the disputed elections of Emperors, deposed Emperors, and brought them humbly to their knees in penance.[2] Under the circumstances of

[1] It is therefore most important in studying the jurisdictional powers of the Church to distinguish carefully between the actions of the Church's authorities as churchmen and as political counsellors and administrators appointed or delegated by the State. Cf. Wernz-Vidal, *Ius Canonicum ad Codicis Norman Exactum,* VI, n. 22.

[2] Pope Innocent I (401-411), for instance, excommunicated Emperor Arcadius (395-408) and Empress Eudoxia (404) for their crimes against St. John Chrysostom. Gregory II (715-731) imposed a synodal anathema against Emperor Leo III, the Isaurion (717-741) for his iconoclasm. Gregory VII (1073-1085) excommunicated Henry IV (1056-1106), and those who were

the times there arose no scandal when the Church extended its temporal activities beyond the limits which seem proper in the modern world.[3]

It was quite natural that during such a period of history the nature of the jurisdiction proper and exclusive to the Church should be questioned, and that the canonists and jurists should split into two camps according as they believed temporal power to constitute or not to constitute an integral part of the divine mission of Peter and his successors.[4]

---

usurping the powers of investiture for bishoprics. Alexander III (1159-1181) excommunicated Frederick I (1152-1190) and Innocent III (1198-1216) anathematized Otto IV, while Frederick II (1212-1250) was confirmed as Emperor by Innocent III in 1215, excommunicated by Gregory IX in 1227, and deposed by Innocent IV in 1245. Cf. Suarez, *Defensio Fidei Catholicae et Apostolicae adversus Anglicanae Sectae Errores,* Lib. III, Cap. XXIII, 7 (hereafter cited *Defensio Fidei*) (Carnegie, *Selections*). Cf. also Carlyle and Carlyle, *A History of Mediaeval Political Theory in the West* (6 vols., New York: Barnes and Noble Inc., 1903-1936), V (hereafter cited *Mediaeval Political Theory*); Cambridge Summer School of Catholic Studies, 1935, *Church and State,* London: Burns, Oates and Washbourne, Ltd., 1936.

3 "The state of society was, moreover, such that the aid of the Church could not be dispensed with and could be replaced by no other. Outside the Church, violence and barbarity, sword and conquest, the untamed powers of nature reigned unchecked, both before the time of Pepin and Charlemagne, and after them under their feeble successors, and indeed long after the complete extinction of the race. . . . Discipline and sound principles could come from the Church alone; and under her influence could the condition of society be improved."—Hergenröther, *Catholic Church and Christian State,* Essay II, Vol. I, 265-6. Cf. also, Hayes, *Political and Social History of Modern Europe* (2 vols. New York: Macmillan, 1920), I, 125.

4 Among those who held that all rights over kingdoms and all powers of dominion were conferred upon Peter as the Vicar of Christ, and that accordingly his successors held supreme temporal power directly and *per se,* according to Suarez and Bellarmine, were: the Gloss, Innocent IV (1243-1254), Hostiensis (1271), Augustinus Triumphus (1243-1328), Oldradus de Laude (1335), Giovanni d'Andrea (1272-1348), Alvarus Pelagius (1350), Bartolus (1314-1359), Paul de Castro (1375-1440), Panormitanus (1386-1453), St. Antoninus (1389-1459), Felinus Sandeus (1444-1503), Sylvester Prierias (1456-1523), Philippus Decius (1454-1537). For listings of these jurists and references to their works, confer Saurez, *Defensio Fidei,* Lib. III, Cap. V, 4 (Carnegie, *Selections*), and also, Bellarmine, *De Romano Pontifice,* Lib. V, Cap. I (*Opera Omnia,* 6 vols. Neapoli, 1851-1862, I, 525).

The medieval relationship between Church and State, Pope and Emperor, reached its ultimate expression under Innocent IV (1243-1254), who summed up his concept of papal power in a letter he wrote at the end of the year 1245 to answer Frederick II's objections against his action of deposition.[5] The popes, as successors of Saint

Among those who held that temporal jurisdiction over all Christians was not possessed by the Pope, according to Suarez and Bellarmine were: Gelasius (492-496), Pope Gregory I (590-604), Pope Nicholas I (858-867), Hugh of St. Victor (1096-1141), Pope Innocent III (1198-1216), St. Bonaventure (1221-1274), Durandus (1237-1296), John of Paris (1306), Petrus Bertandi (1348), John of Turrecremata (1388-1468), Gabriel Biel (ca. 1418-1495), Cajetan (1469-1534), Victoria (1486-1546), Major (1469-1550), Cordubensis (1485-1578), Navarrus (1493-1587). Cf. Suarez, *op. cit.*, Lib. III, Cap. V, 8-9; Bellarmine, *op. cit.*, Lib. V, Cap. I (*Opera Omnia*, 1, 525).

5 "non desistens iuxta solitum apostolica preeminentie vacuare primatum, quem beatum Petrum, fidelium omnium capud, ac successores ipsius accepisse constat, non ab homine, sed a deo cuius auctoritatem profecto diminuit nec deum dei filium heredem universorum et dominium cognoscit, quisquis ab ipsius ditione vicarii se contendit exemptum. Generali namque legatione in terris fungimur regis regum, qui non solum quemcumque, sed ne quid de rebus aut negociis intelligeretur exemptum, sub neutro genere generalius universa complectens, etiam quodcumque ligandi super terram pariter et solvendi apostolorum principi nobisque in ipso plenotudinem tribuit potestatis, etiam ut doctor gentium huiusmodi plenitudinem non restringendam ostenderet, dicens: 'An nescitis, quoniam angelos iudicabimus?' quanto magis secularia! Nonne ad temporalia quoque porrectam exposuit datam eidem in angelos potestatem, ut hiis intelligantur minora subesse, quibus subdita sunt maiora? . . . . Hac potestate usi leguntur plerique pontifices veteris testamenti, qui a nonnullis regibus, qui se indignos fecerant principatu, regni solium auctoritate sibi divinitus tradita transtulerunt. *Relinquitur ergo Romanum pontificem posse saltem casualiter suum exercere pontificale iudicium in quemlibet Christianum cuiuscumque conditionis existit, presertim si de ipso alius iustitie debitum nolit reddere vel non possit, maxime ratione peccati,* ut peccatorem quemcumque, postquam in profundum viciorum venerit per contemptum tamquam publicanum et ethnicum habere constituat et a fidelium corpore alienum sicque *saltem per consequens* privatum, si quam habebat, temporalis regiminis potestate, qui procul dubio extra ecclesiam efferre omin non potesto, cum foris, ubi omnia edificant ad gehennan, a deo nulla sit ordinata potestas. Minus igitur acute persipiunt, nescientes rerum investigare primordia, qui apostolicam sedem autumnant a Constantino principe primitus habuisse imperii principatum, qui prius naturaliter et potencialiter fuisse dinoscitur apud eam. Dominus enim Ihesus Christus, sicut verus homo verusque deus, sic secundum ordinem

Peter, exercised a general "legation" over men in all matters, spiritual and temporal. Since St. Paul had taught that the Church could judge temporal matters because even the judgment of angels was entrusted to the Church, and since the pontiffs of the Old Testament deposed kings, Innocent argued that *a fortiori* the Roman Pontiffs could judge any Christian, no matter what his condition, whenever necessity demanded it (*casualiter*), especially if there was no one else who could or would do so, and most especially if there was involved a question of sin. The result of such a judgment when it inflicted excommunication upon the culprit was the loss of temporal power, for outside the Church there could not exist any legitimate power, inasmuch as all power is ordained by God. The imperial power of

---

Melchisedech verus rex ac verus sacredos existens. . . in apostolica sede non solum pontificalem sed et regalem constituit monarchatum, beato Petro eiusque successoribus terreni simul ac celestis imperii commissis habenis, quod in pluralitate clavium competenter innuitur, ut per unam, quam in spiritualibus super celos accepimus, intelligatur Christi vicarius iudicii potentiam accepisse. Verum idem Constantinus, per fidem Christi catholice incorporatus ecclesie, illam inordinatam tyrampnidem, qua fores antea illegitime utebatur, humiliter ecclesie resignavit. . . et recepit intus a Christi vicario, successore videlicet Christi, ordinatam divinatus imperii potestatem, que deinceps, ad vindictam malorum, laudem vero bonorum, legitime uteretur et, qui prius abutebatur potestate permissa, deinde fungeretur auctoritate concessa. In gremio enim fidelis ecclesie ambo gladii habentur administrationis utriusque reconditi. . . . Neuter quoque non creditur iuris Petri, cum de materiali eidem dominus non dixerit 'abice,' sed 'converte gladium tuum,' ut ipsum videlicet per te ipsum ultra non exerceas, 'in vaginam.' Tuum gladium tamque vaginam signantius, ut apud suum vicarium, capud ecclesie militantis, etsi non executionem huius gladii divino ei prohibitam interdicto, auctoritatem tamen, et qua eadem executio producitur, in legis ministerium, malorum vindicem bonorumque tutorem innueret residere. Huius siquidem materialis potestas gladii apud ecclesiam est implicata, sed per imperatorem, qui eam inde recipit, explicatur et que in sinu ecclesie potentialis est solummodo et inclusa, fit cum transfertur in principem, actualis. Hoc nempe ille ritus ostendit, quo summus pontifex cessari, quem coronat, exhibet gladium vagina contentum, quem acceptum princeps exerit, et vibrando innuit se illius exercitium accepisse."—(Italics added). This letter, contained in E. Winkleman, *Acta Imperii inedita Saeculi XIII, XIV* (1880-1885), Vol. II, 1035, 1 (p. 697, 1, 32 f.), was inaccessible to the writer. He quotes it from the footnotes of the scholarly work of the Carlyles, *Mediaeval Political Theory,* V, 308-9.

the pope derived not as a gift from Constantine, as some erroneously held, but through the bestowal of the keys upon Peter. The political power which Constantine exercised before his conversion was illegitimate and tyrannical. He therefore humbly resigned it to the Church in order to receive it back again as duly ordered to God. Innocent again repeated the allegory of the two swords, through which the relationship of the spiritual and temporal powers was commonly expressed during the Middle Ages.[6] In the Garden of Gethsemani Peter was not told to cast away his sword (temporal power). He was told to sheathe it (*"converte gladium tuum"*), not to use it himself, but nevertheless to retain it. The temporal power was therefore contained implicitly, or in principle, in the papal mission, but in practice, and actually, it was exercised by the Emperor, who received it from the pope in the symbolical ceremony of consecration.

B. *The Judicial Power of the Church in the Ages of Christendom*

As was to be expected with such a social-political framework as that of the turbulent ages of Christendom, the judicial function of the Church was of wide scope and power. Specifically, the Church as a spiritual society was considered to be superior in nature to the civil society.[7] The power of the Pope, as Vicar of Christ on earth, was supreme and entirely independent,[8] and the Pope was consequently the supreme judge on earth, and so beyond the jurisdictional powers of any human judges, in the tradition not only of the Apostles, but also of Constantine.[9] The emperor, on the other hand, was subject,

---

[6] Cf. Luke, 22:37-8; Matthew, 26:51-4; Innocentius III, *Regesta,* III, 3, col. 171; VII, 212, col. 871; XV, 189, col. 711 (*MPL,* Vols, 214-216; numbered according to the years of his pontiticate: 1198-1213). For a complete study of the development of this doctrine consult Volume V of *Mediaeval Political Theory.*

[7] Its superiority was as "the sun to the moon," (Innocent III, *Regesta,* I, 401, col. 377); as "gold to lead" (c. 10, D. CXVII).

[8] "Suscipitisne libertatem uerbi? Libenter accipitis, quod lex Christi sacerdotali uos subiicit potestati atque istis tribunalibus subdit? Dedit enim et nobis potestatem, dedit principatum multo perfectiorem principatibus uestris. Aut numquid iustum uobis uidetur, si cedat spiritus carni, si a terrenis celestia superentur, si diuinis preferantur humana?—c. 6, D. X.

[9] "Nemini est de sedis apostolicae judicio judicare."—c. 30, C. XVII, q. 4; "Numquam de pontificibus nisi ecclesiam iudicasse,"—c. 12, D. XCVI;

in all things which concerned the spiritual, to the ecclesiastical judiciary,[10] and it was his duty to defend the Church, particularly by suppressing heresy.[11] While strictly temporal matters, such as feudal disputes, were ordinarily left to the secular authority, as was proper *de iure*,[12] doubtful questions of competency were to be decided by the spiritual authority as the superior society.[13] In a complex case, for instance, one involving the property of a cleric or a church, and of a

---

Gratian also quoted from a letter of Pope Nicholas (865); "Denique hi, quibus tantum humanis rebus, et non divinis praesse permissum est, quomodo de his, per quos divina ministrantur, iudicare presumant, penitus ignoramus," —*Ibid.*, c. 5; concerning Constantine, cf. *ibid.*, c. 8.

[10] "Sed forsan dicetur, quod aliter cum regibus, et aliter cum aliis est agendum. Ceterum scriptum novimus in lege divina: 'Ita magnum iudicabis, ut parvum, nec erit apud te acceptio personarum.' "—Innocentius III, c. 13, X, *de iduiciis*, II, 1; "Si imperator Catholicus est . . . filius est, non presul ecclesiae; . . . ad sacerdotes enim Deus voluit que ecclesiae sunt disponenda pertinere, vos subiicit potestati atque istis tribunalibus subdit. . ."—c. 11, D. XCVI; cc. 1, 3, 4, 5, 10, D. X.

[11] "Sometimes secular princes have held pre-eminent powers within the Church for the purpose of safeguarding ecclesiastical discipline. For the rest, such powers within the Church would not be necessary, except that what the clergy cannot very well effect through doctrinal instruction, the civil authority accomplishes through fear of punishment. Frequently the heavenly kingdom is aided by the earthly kingdom to the extent that those within the Church who offend in doctrinal and disciplinary matters are brought under subjection by the vigor of their rulers. Likewise, this power of princes lays upon the necks of the proud forms of discipline that the Church cannot employ to advantage. . . Let secular princes know that they must render an account to God regarding matters concerning the Church, the guardianship of which they receive from Christ. For whether Catholic princes have increased or have diminished the peace and discipline of the Church, God demands an account of those to whose power He has entrusted His Church."—c. 20, C. XXIII, q. 5, as translated in Cicognani, *Canon Law*, pp. 121-122; cf. also, c. 18, *Non frustra*, C. XXIII, q. 5.

[12] "Non enim intendimus iudicare de feudo, cuius ad ipsum spectat iudicium, nisi forte iure commune per speciale privilegium vel contrariam consuetudinem aliquid sit distractum."—Innocentius III, c. 13, X, *de iudiciis*, II; "Vasallus coram domino feudi conveniendus est, etiamsi dominus feudi sit ecclesiastica persona, dummodo ibi actor possit suam iustitiam consequi; alias loci ordinarius poterit adiri. . ." c. 6, X, *de iudiciis*, II, 1.

[13] C. 13, *Per venerabilem*, X, *qui filii sint legitimi*, IV, 17; cf. *Mediaeval Political Theory*, II, 232-5.

layman, it was the Pope who decided that the cleric, acting as plaintiff, must sue in a civil court on the principle that the plaintiff must follow the forum of the defendant.[14]

While a precursory survey could seem to indicate that the medieval Church at times far over-reached its legitimate judicial jurisdiction, a closer study of the carefully defined grounds which governed such cases reveals that the canonists called upon the spiritual authority of the Church with a view to counterbalancing the ineffectiveness of the medieval secular powers in the interest of justice, peace, and public welfare.

Innocent IV, under whom as a noted canonist, the power of the Papacy achieved its high-water mark, illustrated this point.[15] Certainly if the mediëval Church, like a torrential flood, had raged beyond the channels of its due course, sweeping away all lawful secular power before it, the muddy traces of that now receded rampage would be evident in the canonical works of this Pope, who stated that in principle and theory the jurisdiction of the Church extended over all men, even the un-baptized, by reason of the absolute power of God the Creator.[16] Actually, however, his *Commentaries on the Decretals* recognize this power to be potential rather than practical, and placed

---

14 Alexander III, c. 5, X, *de iudiciis*, II, 2.

15 The Carlyles note that a consideration of the extreme theory of the later thirteenth century must begin with an examination of the principles set out by Innocent IV, who developed the conclusions implicit in the doctrines of Innocent III, and who was the main source and inspiration for the doctrines of the canonists of the later thirteenth century, such as Hostiensis and William Durandus. The principles of Innocent IV relative to Church and State are to be found in his *Commentaria in V Libros Decretalium* (Venetiis, 1552) [hereafter cited *Commentaria*], rather than in his decretals, for Innocent IV continued his work as a canonist even in the papacy, so that in his decrees he issued judgments and dogmatic statements, while in his *Commentaria* he simply set forth his opinion as a canonist. Cf. *Mediaeval Political Theory*, pp. 318-9.

16 "Deus creavit in principio coelam et terram et omnia quae in eis sunt, angelicam et humanam naturam, spiritualia et temporalia, ipsaque per seipsum rexit, sicut factor suam rem gubernat . . . usque ad Christum qui fuit naturalis dominus et Rex noster . . . et ipse Jesus Christus vicarium suum constituit Petrum et successores suos . . ."—Innocentius IV, *Commentaria*, ad c. 9, X, *de foro competenti*, II, 2.

stringent restrictions on the exercise of any such jurisdiction.[17] They further limit the right of an ecclesiastical judge to involve himself in matters pertaining to secular jurisdiction to eleven specific grounds.[18]

1. Vacancy of the Emperor's Throne

Because of the intimate relationship between Pope and Emperor, "the one the consecrator and examiner, the other the sworn advocate and recipient," the temporal power was considered as returning to the hands that had bestowed it, whenever the Emperor's throne became vacant. Though this title to interim power was predicated primarily upon the peculiar circumstances of medieval politics, it was not the sole reason for validating this ground of competence. In the absence of the normal temporal authority which ruled Christendom, the Church was the only legitimate and recognized authority which could effectively maintain public welfare, peace, and order in the international Christian society. Moreover, such circumstances could not but produce ill effects upon the spiritual as well as upon the temporal order. It was, indeed, in view of the spiritual welfare of

[17] "Bene tamen credimus quod Papa qui est vicarius Jesus Christi, potestatem habet, non tantum super Christianos, sed etiam super omnes infideles; cum enim Christus habuerit super omnes potestatem, unde in Psalmo, *Deus iudicium tuum regi da* . . . Omnes autem tam fideles quam infideles oves sunt Christi, per creationem, licet non sint de ovili ecclesiae. Et sic per praedicta apparent quod Papa super omnes habet iurisdictionem et potestatem *de iure, licet non de facto*. Unde per hanc potestatem quam habet Papa credo quod si gentilis, qui non habet legem nisi naturae, si contra legem naturae facit, potest licite puniri per Papam. Argumentum Gen. 19, ubi habes, quod sodomitas, qui contra legem naturae peccabunt, puniti sunt a Deo; cum autem Dei judicio sunt nobis exemplaria, non video quare Papa, qui est vicarius Christi, hoc non possit, et etiam dummodo facultas adsit, et idem dico si colant idola. Naturale enim est unum et solum Deum creaturam colere, et non creaturas. Item Judaeos potest iudicare Papa, si contra legem Evangelii faciunt in moralibus, si eorum prelati eos non puniunt, et eodem modo si heres circa suam legem inveniant."—Innocentius IV, *Commentaria,* ad c. 8, X, *de vote et voti redemptione,* III, 34.

[18] C. 9, X, *De foro competenti,* II, 2. Since these eleven grounds were elaborated at the height of the medieval period, and since they receive mention in a volume which, written by one of the most noted canonists of the time, comments on the preceding legislation of this period, they thus provide a valid guide for an examining of the question regarding the competence of the Church courts under Christendom.

men and society, and on the basis of supplementing for the failure of secular power, that the Pope, through "the plenitude of power which he held as Vicar of Christ," carried out this function in the case of kings other than the Emperor, over whom he held no power of consecration or of appointment.

Moreover, in the case of vacant kingdoms, ecclesiastical judges were forbidden to intervene unless they first were petitioned according to the procedure of denunciation as described in the decretal *Novit,* i.e., according to the evangelical procedure of *dic ecclesiae.*[19] The Church thus remained aloof from secular matters until all secular power, private as well as public, had failed, and an appeal for aid was submitted.

Even a further limitation was noted by Innocent. Cases of rebellion against the Emperor, if they were so serious in nature as to destroy his ability to maintain justice, did not constitute a vacancy of the throne which would allow papal intervention. In such cases it became incumbent upon the Pope to assist the Emperor in quashing the rebellion, and thereby restore due temporal authority.

2. Negligence of Secular Judges

If the first grounds for ecclesiastical judicial action in temporal affairs was based on the inability of the secular powers to administer justice, the second, based on the negligence of these powers, was also supplementary in character. The episcopal courts were not to interfere in temporal cases *ad libitum.* If the negligent secular judge was subordinate to the Emperor, or to any other secular superior, jurisdiction devolved not upon the Pope, but upon the proximately higher temporal authority. Only in cases in which an injured party could not obtain justice from the temporal authority was it permissible for him to sue before the ecclesiastical courts. When such cases did arise the status of the injured party was abstracted from, for even nobles and the wealthy could suffer injustice under such circumstances.

In the year 1205 there occurred in Ireland a case in which the Pope intervened in a temporal dispute, because no secular authority either could, or would, render justice. A certain John de Courcey

---

19 Cf. *supra,* pp. 13-15; and *infra,* pp. 49-50.

submitted a bill of complaint to Innocent III against a nobleman of that country, named Hugh Lacey. Lacey had invaded his lands, taken him prisoner, and then given him a choice between death and the forfeiting of his lands and possessions, along with exile from Ireland with an oath never to return. Naturally enough, De Courcey chose the latter course, and then from exile appealed to the Pope to release him from his oath and to restore his lands. Innocent was thus provided with the double grounds of a direct jurisdiction over the oath and of a devolved jurisdiction in consequence of the unwillingness of secular authorities to administer justice. Accordingly, Innocent ordered the Bishop of Armagh to investigate the case, and, if the charge proved true, to order Lacey to restore the lands under penalty of excommunication.[20]

3 and 4. Defense of the Weak and Unfortunate

The third and fourth grounds by which Innocent IV extended the judicial power of the Church over temporal affairs pertained to laymen who, because of their weakness and resourcelessness, found it particularly difficult to obtain justice in the civil courts.

First among these unfortunates were the widows, for whom the Church had always felt a special concern and duty.[21] The Church, however, willingly bestowed jurisdiction over widows upon the secular authority, and the ecclesiastical judge was forbidden once again, to proceed unless the temporal courts failed to render justice.[22] Examples of this solicitude for the welfare of widows are furnished by Innocent III (1198-1216) who intervened to force King John of England (1199-1216) to carry out his agreement concerning the

---

20 Innocentius III, *Regesta,* VIII, 114, cols. 681-2.

21 Innocent III wrote, "If a judge, even when he fears neither God nor man, feels concern over a case involving a widow, . . . how could it be possible for us not to hear the cries of widows, when we, though unworthily, are the Vicar on earth of Him Who renders judgment for all who suffer, without respect for persons, and Who by prophetic voice commands aid for the oppressed and defense for the widow?"—*Ibid.,* VII, cols. 475-6; cf. also c. 1, D. LXXXVII.

22 "Papa habet iurisdictionem supra viduas, sed si de gratia defert iudicibus saecularibus, ut non procedat iudex ecclesiasticus nisi propter negligentiam laici iudicis."—Innocentius IV, *Commentaria* ad c. 11, X, *de foro competenti,* II, 2.

dowry rights of the widow of Richard I (1189-1199),[23] and ordered the princes of Germany to release Sibylla, a noblewoman, and widow of Tancred of Sicily, her son and daughters, and other captives from Sicily under pain of ecclesiastical penalties.[24]

The fourth instance of ecclesiastical competency given by Innocent IV concerns legal aid for the poor, and had its precedent in the Council of Toledo in the year 400.[25] Orphans and wards were also included in the category of persons who could seek ecclesiastical legal aid.[26]

5. Hard and Doubtful Matters which could not be definitely Settled by Secular Judges

> If thou perceive that there be among you a hard and doubtful matter in judgment between blood and blood, cause and cause, leprosy and leprosy; and thou see that the words of the judges within the gates vary: arise, and go up to the place, which the Lord thy God shall choose. And thou shalt come to the priests of the Levitical race, and to the judge, that shall be at that time: and thou shalt ask of them, and they shall shew thee the truth of the judgment. And thou shalt do whatsoever they shall say, that preside in that place, which the Lord shall choose, and what they shall teach thee, according to his law; and thou shalt follow their sentence: . . . But he that will be proud, and refuse to obey the commandment of the priest. . . and the decree of the judge, that man shall die, and thou shalt take away the evil from Israel.[27]

This ground for ecclesiastical jurisdiction, based on the laws of the Old Testament, was, as in the preceding instances, motivated by the wish to supplement for the defects of the secular courts, and established the papal court as the supreme court of appeals whenever a question was so difficult or ambiguous that the secular courts were at

---

23 ". . . quia viduis et orphanis specialiter sumus in sua debitores, tuae saluti potius consulentes. . . abbatibus dedimus mandata, ut ipsi te ad restitutionem . . . et ad iustitiam super dote . . . coram eis poenarium exhibendum, monitione praemissa, per districtionem ecclesiasticam, appellatione remota compellant. . . ."—Innocentius III, *Regesta,* VI, 194, col. 220.

24 *Ibid.,* I, 26, cols. 20-1.

25 C. 21, C. XXIV, q. 3.

26 Cf. c. 2, D. LXXXVII; c. 26, C. XXIII, p. 5.

27 *Deuteronomy,* 17:8-12.

variance, and thus no definitive decision could be obtained. In asserting this ground for competence Innocent IV was thus merely following the precedent of Innocent III, who applied this law of the Old Testament to justify his right to judge at least indirectly and *per consequentiam* the civil side of an involved case of legitimation.[28]

Applied to the New Testament, the "place which the Lord thy God shall choose," was the Apostolic See, and "He that will . . . refuse to obey. . . the decree of the judge, that man shall die, and thou shalt take away the evil from Israel," was applied to mean that whoever treated this sentence with contempt was to be excommunicated, and so considered as dead and separated from the communion of the faithful. Innocent IV analyzed the three types of cases mentioned in this law. He interpreted the "judgment between blood and blood" as meaning a case in which the accused spilt blood, and therefore some civil crime, such as homicide, adultery, robbery, and the like; the judgment between "leprosy and leprosy" as meaning the leprosy of heresy, and therefore some ecclesiastical crimes such as simony and sacrilege; and the judgment between "cause and cause" as meaning a contractual suit or dispute regarding the patronal rights over a church, so that contentious actions of either a civil or an ecclesiastical nature were included. Innocent concluded, therefore, that all actions, criminal and contentious, ecclesiastical or civil, were to be referred to the Apostolic See when they were so difficult and ambiguous as to draw nothing but conflicting decisions in the civil courts.

6. The Temporal Power of the Pope in Rome and in the Papal States

Since the Pope was a temporal as well as a spiritual ruler, his courts naturally handled the temporal affairs of his domains. In *caput* 7 of his titles on appeals, Innocent, however, forbade any appeal to the ecclesiastical court, either prior to or following a trial by a civil judge, unless the litigants were subject to his temporal jurisdiction, and he revoked the necessity of making such appeals in any place outside his jurisdiction where that custom might have existed.

---

[28] Innocent III, in the famous decretal, "*Per venerabilem*" (c. 13, X, *qui filii sint legitimi*, IV, 17).

7. Appeal according to the Evangelical Process of *Dic Ecclesiae*

> If thy brother shall offend against thee, go and rebuke him between thee and him alone. If he shall hear thee, thou shalt gain thy brother. If he will not hear thee, take with thee one or two more, that in the mouth of two or three witnesses every word may stand; and if he will not hear them, tell the Church. And if he will not hear the Church, let him be to thee as the heathen and publican.[29]

For a second time the Holy Bible furnished a text upon which to establish ecclesiastical competency. Once again the motive was the providing of relief not offered by the civil courts, for in discussing this ground Innocent IV stated: "This manner of proceeding has its place wherever something of a temporal nature must be given or done because of a natural obligation for which no civil or canonical action provides redress, as when someone has pledged to give or to do something without a stipulation. In this case the denunciation is to be used because it pertains to the Pope to judge all mortal sins." [30]

This was the ground on which Innocent III intervened in the feudal dispute between John of England (1199-1216) and Philip Augustus of France (1180-1223). The Pope ordered a cease-fire under threat of ecclesiastical punishment, and Philip retorted that the Pope had no business interfering in feudal disputes. The Pope responded with two letters, one to Philip, dated October 31, 1203, and a second to the clergy of France in April, 1204. The second is the famous letter, *Novit,* in which the Pope stated that he had no intention of usurping power which did not belong to him. Feudal disputes did, indeed, belong to the temporal forum, but he had not directly concerned himself with that question. He had demanded that Philip make peace. His jurisdiction for doing so was based first on his duty as that of the Pope, to seek peace, and secondly on the fact that the case had been submitted to him by John who, in following the evangelical procedure of *dic ecclesiae,* had charged Philip with having sinned against him. Since this matter touched the question of sin, the Pope had indisputable judicial competence. Moreover, there was involved also

---

[29] Matthew, 18:15-17; also cf. *supra,* pp. 13-15.

[30] Innocentius IV, *Commentaria* ad c. 13, X, *de iudiciis,* II, 1; jurisdiction over persons incriminated with mortal sin is discussed below, pp. 53-55.

question of broken oaths, which furnished yet another basis for papal jurisdiction.[31]

8. Relief from Suspect Judges

The eighth ground listed by Innocent aimed at providing justice for those who, because of the prejudice or subornation of secular judges, could not obtain justice in the civil courts. To explain this point Innocent referred to the case in which the civil officials of Vercelli, who, when charges had been brought against them offered to lay aside their jurisdiction, and asked for ecclesiastical intervention

---

[31] "Non ergo putet aliquis, quod iurisdictionem aut potestatem illustris regis Francorum perturbare aut minuere intendamus. . . . Sed quum Dominus dicat in evangelio, 'si peccaverit in te frater tuus . . . dic ecclesiae . . .' . . . et rex Angliae, sicut asserit, sit paratus sufficienter ostendere, quod rex Francorum peccat in ipsum, et ipse circa eum in correctione processit secundam regulam evangelicam, et tandem, quia nullo modo profecit, dixit ecclesiae: quomodo nos, qui summus ad regimen universalis ecclesiae superna dispositione vocati, mandatum divinum possumus non exaudire, ut non procedamus secundum formam ipsius, nisi forsitan ipse coram nobis vel legato nostro sufficientem in contrarium rationem ostendat? Non enim intendimus iudicare de feudo, cuius ad ipsum spectat iudicium, nisi forte iure commune per speciale privilegium vel contrariam consuetudinem aliquid sit detractum, sed decernere de peccato, cuius ad nos pertinet sine dubitatione censura, quam in quemlibet exercere possumus et debemus. . . . Quum enim non humanae constitutioni, sed divinae legi potius innitamur, Nostra quia potestas non est ex homine, sed ex Deo; nullus, qui sit sanae mentis, ignorat, quin ad officium nostrum spectet de quocunque mortale peccato corripere quemlibet Christianum, et, si correctionem contempserit, ipsum per districtionem ecclesiasticum coercere. . . Sed forsan dicetur, quod aliter cum regibus, et aliter cum aliis est agendum. Ceterum scriptum novimus in lege divina; 'Ita magnum iudicabis, ut parvum, nec erit apud te acceptio personarum' . . . Licet autem hoc modo procedere valeamus super quolibet criminali peccato, ut peccatorem revocemus a vitio ad virtutem, ab errore ad veritatem, praecipue tamen quem contra pacem peccatur, quae est vinculum caritatis. . . Postremo quum inter reges ipsos reformata fuerint pacis foedera, et utrinque praestito proprio iuramento firmata, quae tamen usque ad tempus praetaxatum servata non fuerint, numquid non poterimus de iuramenti religione cognoscere, quod ad iudicium ecclesiae non est dubium pertinere, ut rupta pacis foedera reformentur."—c. 13, *novit*, X, *de iudiciis*, II, 1; Innocentius III, *Regesta*, VII, 64, col. 326; c. 13, X, *de judiciis*, II, 1; the letter of 1203 is contained in the *Regesta*, VI, 163, col. 177-180. Cf. Cappello, *Summa Iuris Publici Ecclesiastici*, n. 224.

under the pretext of affording the plaintiffs more equitable justice. Alexander III, however, saw that their underlying motive was that of harassing and burdening the plaintiffs with added labor and expense. Accordingly Alexander ordered the Bishop to refuse such a petition, lest real justice be denied, especially since the dispute was of a secular nature, and justice could and would be afforded by the secular courts. In the event that the plaintiffs themselves appealed because they felt themselves discriminated against by these same consuls, it would be possible to entertain their appeal, especially if this should occur during the vacancy of the throne when it would be impossible to appeal to superior secular judges. If the judges were suspect, this question was to be settled first by means of an arbitration on the part of judges agreed upon by both litigants, and only if the charge of suspicion was verified could recourse be had to the papal or episcopal court.[32]

9. Things Annexed to the Spiritual

The ninth ground given by Innocent looked to the intimate nature of, and balance between, spiritual and temporal matters as preventing an air-tight exclusion of the one class or group from the other. There were temporal affairs which were intimately bound up with the spiritual, such as church property, income, donations to the poor, care of the sick. There were also spiritual affairs which evinced temporal aspects, such as benefices and patronal rights.

The most common example, and perhaps the most practical, of the medieval canonists was that of marriage and its consequences. Since matrimony was a sacrament, and inasmuch as God had said, "What God has joined together, let no man tear asunder," matrimony could be judged not by man, but by the Vicar of God alone.[33] Any case which directly touched the sacramental bond, or depended upon the validity of the sacrament, thereby demanding a judgment regarding the validity of the marriage, was, accordingly, subject to the exclusive jurisdiction of the Church.

The question of legitimacy was a primary example. This question depended directly on the valid character of the marriage of the

---

[32] C. 10, X, *de foro competenti,* II, 2.

[33] Innocentius IV, *Commentaria* ad c. 3, X, *de ordine cognitionum,* II, 10.

parents, and so Innocent, along with all the medieval canonists, ruled that the question of natal legitimacy was a spiritual one, and so belonged to the exclusive jurisdiction of the ecclesiastical judge, whether it arose as the principal point at issue, or as an incidental question, or even as an exception, and this was true even if the question arose after death.[34]

As an illustration of how the question of illegitimacy could easily arise as an incidental issue, and yet be entirely prejudicial to the major dispute, there was the case of the questioned right of succession to the court of Campania in the year 1223. Since this right depended upon the natal status of the future queen, Pope Honorius (1216-1227) wrote to Louis VIII of France (1223-1226), asking him not to proceed in this case until the Church had completed its investigation, and rendered a decision on this point, lest the affair become complicated by diverse processes, and embroil the judicial order in a state of resultant confusion.[35]

The granting of a dispensation for legitimation was not of itself a judicial question, but the result of a judicial finding. While the Church could legitimate a person in spiritual affairs, v.g., for promotion to sacred orders, there was some discussion among the canonists whether or not ecclesiastical legitimation would automatically legitimize a person in the civil forum, even though he was not subject to the temporal authority of the Church.[36]

The question of inheritance, being a temporal affair, was subject to the secular courts.[37] If, however, the king insisted on the settlement of this question in his courts, but the decision depended upon the prejudicial question of legitimacy, which belonged to the Church, then there was the danger that there might arise an absurdity and an intolerable contradiction in which, e.g., the Church pronounced a judgment of illegitimacy, and the State a judgment of inheritance.[38] Therefore in the Church's decision in cases of legitimacy, it sometimes directed the litigants not to proceed with the civil question of

---

[34] *Loc. cit.*, and ad c. 5, X, *qui filii sint legitimi*, IV, 17.

[35] C. 3, X, *de foro competenti*, II, 2.

[36] *Per venerabilem*—c. 13, X, *qui filii sint legitimi*, IV, 17.

[37] Innocentius IV, *Commentaria*, ad c. 9, X, *de foro competenti*, II, 2.

[38] Innocentius IV, *Commentaria*, ad c. 3, X, *de ordine cognitionum*, II, 10.

inheritance, but to consider the person an heir or to repudiate that status, in accordance with the Church's decision on legitimacy.[39] Such a papal injunction was justified, not only because of the intimate relationship between the spiritual and the temporal factors, but because of the sin of injustice which was involved.[40] In spite of this, it seems that it was the general procedure to submit the question of temporalities to the civil authorities upon the completion of the ecclesiastical procedure.[41]

Patronal rights were judged to be so connected with the spiritual that they belonged entirely to the judgment of the Church.[42] Innocent IV added likewise the questions regarding burial, for though laymen indeed possessed burial rights, still the ownership of the sepulchres did not pertain to them.[43] To cover all such contingencies, Innocent IV laid down the general principle that a lay judge had no authority to try a spiritual case, whether it arose as the principal point at issue, or incidentally, or as a counter-suit.[44]

10. Sinful Actions

Innocent III had stated, "No one of sound mind is ignorant that it is our duty to correct every Christian for any mortal sin whatsoever, and, if he shows contempt for our correction, to bring force

---

[39] C. 1, X, *qui filii sint legitimi,* IV, 17.

[40] Cf. *glossa ordinaria,* ad c. 1, X, *qui filii sint legitimi,* IV, 17; Innocentius IV, *op. cit.,* c. 9, X, *de foro competenti,* II, 2.

[41] ". . . si eadem possessione fuisset per violentiam spoliatus; nos attendentes, quod ad regem pertinet, non ad ecclesiam, de talibus possessionibus iudicare, ne videamur iuri et dignitati. . . Henrici regis, Anglorum principis, detrahere . . . mandamus, quatenus regi possessionum iudicium relinquentes, de causa principali, vidilicet utrum mater praedicti R. de legitimo sit matrimonio nata, plenius cognoscatis, et causam huiusmodi. . . terminetis." —c. 7, X, *qui filii sint legitimi,* IV, 17; cf. also note 37, p. 52.

[42] "Causa vero iuris patronatus ita coniuncta est et connexa cum spiritualibus causis, quod non nisi ecclesiastico iudicio valeat definiri, et apud ecclesiasticum iudicem solummodo terminari."—Alexander III to the King of England, c. 3, X, *de iudiciis,* II, 1; cf. also *glossa ordinaria* on the words *iudicem ecclesiasticum,* c. 11, X, *de foro competenti,* II, 2.

[43] Innocentius IV, *Commentaria,* c. 2, X, *de ordine cognitionum,* II, 10.

[44] ". . . dicitur generaliter, laicum iudicem de nullo spirituali, nec principaliter, nec incidenter, nec reconveniendo, posse cognoscere."—*ibid.,* c. 3, X, *de ordine cognitionum,* II, 10.

upon him by means of ecclesiastical judicial action." [45] Oftentimes, then, if the Church could not exercise jurisdiction over the contentious elements in a temporal dispute for any of the above mentioned grounds, the commission of sin in the case brought the dispute at least indirectly under the Church's jurisdiction.[46] It was in this fashion that Innocent III intervened in the feudal dispute between Kings John and Philip Augustus, stating that he did not intend to judge the feudal dispute, which was the function of secular authorities, but to judge the sin that was involved.[47] It was likewise through the breaking of the pledge or the oath under which contracts were made, that the Church obtained indirect jurisdiction over contractual disputes, though the sin of fraud, especially if it concerned the Church or resulted in the oppression of the poor, proved in itself sufficient as a reason for ecclesiastical intervention.[48]

Innocent IV listed the crimes of breaking the peace, of committing perjury, simony, or sacrilege, of perpetrating usury, of heresy, and of embarking upon a matrimonial separation because of adultery, as belonging to the jurisdiction of the Church.[49] All of these crimes were treated in detail by the canonists, and there were included such regulations as: those who commit perjury, or perpetrate any criminal act, and through fear of a long penance refuse to confess, are to be excommunicated as *vitandi*,[50] as also are those who have engaged in blasphemous swearing.[51] The whole fourth question of the seventeenth *Causa* of Gratian's *Decretum* was given over to a treatment of sacrilege. This crime related, among others, to those who stole from the Church, alienated its faculties, arrested a bishop, unless judgment against him had been rendered canonically, or presumed to exercise judgment over the Apostolic See.[52] C. 3, C. XII, q. 2, stated that no one could rightfully ignore the fact that anything which was consecrated to God, whether a man, or a beast, or a field,

[45] C. 13, *novit*, X, *de iudiciis*, II, 1; cf. footnote 31, p. 50.

[46] Cf. Innocentius IV, *Commentaria*, ad c. 13, X, *de iudiciis*, II, 1.

[47] Cf. the decretal *novit*, quoted in footnote 31, p. 50.

[48] Innocentius IV, *Commentaria*, ad c. 8, X, *de foro competenti*, II, 2.

[49] *Commentaria*, ad c. 13, X, *iudiciis*, II, 1.

[50] C. 17, C. XXII, q. 1.

[51] C. 10, C. XXII, q. 1.

[52] Cc. 5, 17, 22, 30.

or any other thing, once it had been consecrated, was a holy of holies for God, and pertained as a right to priests. It was therefore inexcusable for anyone to pillage, take away, lay waste to, invade, or steal such things which pertained to God and to the Church. Until reparation and satisfaction had been made to the Church, such a person was to be judged as guilty of sacrilege, and if he was unwilling to make reparation, he was to be excommunicated.[53]

Although those who injured the Church were ordinarily tried by secular judges on the principle that the plaintiff followed the forum of the defendant, yet, because of the sacrilegious nature of the crime, and in consequence of the probable negligence of the secular judges, such persons could be tried in the ecclesiastical court.[54] The sentence of the ecclesiastical judge had the force of annulling transactions in which church goods were alienated contrary to ecclesiastical regulations, even though there existed a written contract.[55]

Foremost among the sins over which the power of the Church extended was that of the breaking of the peace. In one case in which Innocent III used this ground, he explained the sinful nature of aggression by stating, "Since love is the fullness of the law, according to the Apostle, so dissension constitutes a transgression of the divine law." [56] It was the attempt of Boniface VIII (1294-1303) to arbitrate peace between England, France, and Germany, on this very ground, that occasioned the disastrous rebellion of the arrogant Philip the Fair (1285-1314).[57]

---

[53] Cf. also, c. 4, C. XII, q. 2; c. 57, C. XVI, q. 1; c. 21, C. XXIV, q. 3.

[54] "Malefactores ecclesiarum in utroque foro conveniri possunt—Rubrica. "Quum sit generale, ut actor forum rei sequatur, conveniens est, ut apud iudices saeculares raptores prius conveniantur. Sed si iustitiam exhibere contempserint aut iudices ex quacumque causa fuerint negligentes, quia iudicandi sunt sacrilegi ab ecclesia, de crimini illo censuram poteris in eos ecclesiasticam exercere. Verum quoniam saeculares iudices in exhibenda iustitia personis ecclesiasticis saepe in iudicio sunt remissi, iam per consuetudinem in favorem ecclesiae est introductum, ut malefactores suos, qui sacrilegi sunt censendi, venerabilium locorum rectores possint sub quo maluerint judice convenire."—c. 8, X, *de foro competenti,* II, 2.

[55] C. 13, C. XII, q. 2.

[56] Innocentius III, *Regesta,* II, 39, col. 580.

[57] *Mediaeval Political Theory,* V, 374-398.

11. Lay Servants of the Clergy, and Those Holding Administrative Functions in the Church

As the ninth ground had drawn within the ambit of ecclesiastical jurisdiction temporal things and affairs which were connected with the Church, so this final ground extends the *privilegium fori* by way of interparticipation [58] to men who, although not clerical or religious in character or in their state of life, nevertheless were engaged in the work of the Church and its clergy.[59] The extension of this privilege in this manner was not novel. It had its precedents in Gregory in 599, and in the Council of Toledo in 400, while as recently as 1198 Innocent III had extended it to include the Crusaders during their travels.[60]

It was also judged more fitting for those who were performing solemn penance to refrain from using the secular courts, though they were not absolutely forbidden to do so.[61]

If these eleven grounds of Innocent IV seem to some to be somewhat excessive, the medieval Church must not be judged too harshly. In times when the adolescent states could not always provide justice, the Church stood alone as a buttress of justice, and a shield for the weak. Outside of Italy its judicial activity entered into temporal fields only occasionally, *casualiter,* for spiritual motives, and only when the public welfare or justice demanded, and then only after all due secular power had failed.

The scholarly Carlyles sum up their admirable thirty years of historic research on this period with the following judgment:

> It is possible to suggest that Hildebrand and Innocent III may have sometimes dreamed of a theocracy, may have at least thought of a world directed, and, if need be, ruled by the representative of the Spiritual Power. But if they did so it was but a dream, not necessarily an ignoble dream, but it had no relation to the

[58] Concerning the interparticipation in privileges, cf. cans. 63-65.

[59] Cf. c. 69, C. XII, q. 2; c. 5, D. LXXXIX.

[60] Innocentius III, *Regesta,* I, 300, col. 261.

[61] "Aliud quidem est debita iusta reposcere, aliud propria perfectionis amore contempnere. Sed illicitorum veniam postulantem oportet etiam a multis licitis abstinere, dicente Apostolo, 'Omnia mihi licent, sed non omnia expediunt.' Unde si quis penitens habet causam, quam negligere forte non debeat, melius expetet ecclesiasticum quam forense iudicium."—c. 34, C. X I, q. 1.

> actual character of mediaeval society, or to its normal principles. The notion that mediaeval society tended to something like a theocracy is, indeed, not now maintained by any serious student, but it is to be regretted that it still lingers in the popular mind.[62]

According to the testimony of Innocent III himself, "We exercise temporal jurisdiction on occasion, *casualiter,* not that we wish to prejudice another's right, or to usurp to ourselves an undue power, for we are not ignorant of Christ's response in the Gospel, 'Render unto Caesar the things that are Caesar's, and unto God the things that are God's.' "[63]

---

62 *Mediaeval Political Theory,* V. 400.

63 C. 13, *per venerabilem,* X, *qui filii sint legitimi,* IV, 17.

CHAPTER IV

THE AGES OF SECULARISM

A. *The Prelude*

In the very days of Innocent IV, when the judicial activity of the Church had reached its zenith both in theory and in practice, a hostile reaction had already begun to restrict this power. The protests of Frederick II (1212-1250) against his deposition by the Pope stirred a number of French barons to form a compact in November, 1241, swearing that they would not submit any dispute to the judgment of the clergy (some of whom were the sons of slaves), except those pertaining to heresy, marriage, and usury.[1]

In the year 1296 Boniface VIII attempted to bring peace to Europe by forcing a truce upon England, France, and Germany under penalty of excommunication, by right of his jurisdiction over sinful matters. Philip the Fair denied the right of the Pope to intervene in temporal affairs, and, though the arbitration of Boniface was later accepted, it was as a private person, and not as Pope, that he was accepted as mediator. Philip continued to confiscate ecclesiastical revenues and property, to nominate to ecclesiastical offices without canonical provision, and he seized the Papal Representative, the Abbot of Pamiers. Boniface demanded the release of the Abbot,

---

[1] Clerici, "jurisdictionem secularium principium sic absorbent ut filii servorum secundum suas leges judicent liberos et filios liberorum. . . nos omnes regni majores attenti animi percipientes quod regnum non per ius scriptum nec per clericorum arrogantiam, sed per sudores bellicos fuerit acquisitum, presenti decreto omnium juramento statuimus et sancimus ut nullus clericus vel laicus alium de cetero trahat in causam coram ordinario judice vel delegato, nisi super heresi matrimonio vel usuris . . . ut sic jurisdictio nostra ressuscitata respicit, et ipsi hactenus ex nostra depauperatione ditati. . . reducantur ad statum Ecclesie primitive, et in contemplatione viventes . . . ostendant miracula que dudum a seculo recesserunt."—Huillard Breholles, *Historia Diplomatica Frederici Secundi* (1852-1861), VI, 467, as cited in *Mediaeval Political Theory,* V, 313-4.

and in the Bull, *Ausculta, fili carissimi,* on December 5, 1301, remonstrated with Philip for his hostile actions.

When the Bull was presented to the French nobles, Comte d'Artois, Philip's cousin, snatched it away from the papal delegate and threw it into the fire. A forgery was then made, which appealed to the pride of French nationalism by making the Pope say that the king was subject to the Pope in all temporal, as well as spiritual, matters.

In 1302 a synod was held in Rome, following which Boniface VIII published his famous Bull *Unam Sanctam.*[2] The doctrine of the subordination of the one sword to the other was again repeated,[3] and for its basis was furnished the scriptural argument drawn from the statement of St. Paul, "For there is no power but from God, and those that are, are ordained to God" (*Romans,* 13, 1), and the philosophic argument from the subordination of means to ends, and of inferiors to superiors, as found in the order of the universe.

The core of this part of the papal Bull was taken directly from the *De Consideratione* of St. Bernard (1091-1153),[4] who became

[2] ". . . Oportet autem gladium esse sub gladio, et temporalem auctoritatem spirituali subjiici potestati. Nam quum dicat apostolus, 'Non est potestas nisi a Deo, quae autem a Deo sunt, ordinata sunt,' non ordinata essent, nisi gladius esset sub gladio, et tamquam inferior reduceretur per alium in supprema nam secundum beatum Dionysium, lex divinitatis est infima per media, in supprema reduci. Non ergo secundum ordinem universi, omnia eque ac immediate, sed infima per media, inferiora per superiora, ad ordinem reduccuntur. . . . Nam veritate testante, spiritualis potestas terrenam potestatem instituere habet, et judiciare, si bona non fuerit. Sic de ecclesia, et ecclesiastica potestate, verificatur vaticiunium Jeremie 'Ecce constitui te hodie, super gentes et regna,' et cetera quae secuntur. Ergo si deviat terrena potestas judicabitur a potestate spirituale, sed si deviat spiritualis, minor a suo superiore. Si vero suprema a solo Deo, non ab homine poterit judicari, testante, apostolo, 'spiritualis homo iudicat omnia, ipse autem a nemine judicatur.' . . ."—c. 1, *de maioritate et obedientia,* I, 8, in *Extravag. com.*; Potthast, *Regesta Pontificum* (2 vols., Berolini, 1874-1875), n. 2014, (n. 25189).

[3] Cf. footnote 6, p. 41; cf. also Cappello, *Summa Iuris Publici Ecclesiastici,* n. 223.

[4] *De Consideratione,* IV, 2, 2 (*MPL,* CLXXXII, col. 773). Cf. *Rivière Le Problême de l'église et de l'état au Temps de Philippe le Bel* (Paris, Louvain: E. Champion, 1926), for citation of St. Bernard, comparisons with the text of the Bull, and explanation of the role of St. Bernard in this controversy.

the arsenal for the arguments used on both sides in the discussion regarding the temporal power of the Pope. Those who held that temporal jurisdiction does not enter directly into the mission of the Papacy according to the divine plan, and that therefore "the ecclesiastical judge should not investigate or judge concerning sin in temporal matters, but only the secular judge," [5] reinforced their arguments with such statements from St. Bernard as that this work did not belong to the Church, not because the Church was unworthy, but because such work was beneath the station of the Church, which was destined to be occupied with more noble affairs,[6] and also with his admonition, "If you rule the wolves, you will not rule the lambs." [7]

Those who favored the extension of papal power into temporal affairs likewise sought to buttress their position with the doctrine of St. Bernard. Among them was Giles of Rome (ca. 1243-1316). In 1858 Charles Jourdain discovered that Giles was present at the Roman Council of 1302, and that the Bull *Unam Sanctam* was patterned directly upon his *De Ecclesiastica Potestate*,[8] and that Giles in turn had made use *ex professo* of Hugh of St. Victor (1096-1141).[9]

The Bull has been attacked especially for the sentence, *"Spiritualis potestas terrenam postestatem instituere habet,"* because of the connotation that the civil power was merely a delegated power received from the Papacy. Indeed, the text of Hugh of St. Victor reads: *"Nam spiritualis potestas terrenam potestatem et instituere*

---

5 "Et ita de peccato in temporalibus non judicat vel cognoscit judex ecclesiasticus, sed secularis tantum."—John of Paris, *De Potestate Regia et Papalis,* quoted by Rivière, *ibid.,* p. 411.

6 Habent haec infima et terrena judices suos, reges et principes terrae. Quid fines alienos invaditis? Quid falcem vestram in alienam messam extenditis? Non, quia indigni vos, sed quia indignum vobis talibus insistere, quippe potioribus occupatis."—St. Bernard, *De Consideratione,* I, 6, 7 (*MPL,* CLXXXII, cols. 735-6).

7 *De Consideratione,* II, 6, 13 (*MPL,* CLXXXII, col. 749).

8 Giles of Rome, *De Ecclesiastica Potestate,* ed. Oxilia et Boffito, pp. 7-20, quoted and compared with *Unam Sanctam* by Rivière, *op. cit.,* Appendice II, pp. 394-404. Concerning Giles cf. Cambridge Summer School of Catholic Studies, 1935, *Church and State,* pp. 86-7.

9 Hugh of St. Victor, *De Sacramentis,* II, pars II, c. 4 (*MPL,* CLXXVI, col. 418).

habet ut sit, et judicare habet, si bona non fuerit," indicating efficient causality. The *"ut sit"* was not incorporated into the text of *Unam Sanctam.* Whether this was done for the purpose of brevity, or in order not to stir the wrath of Philip too greatly, or for some other reason, is not known. In any event, the omission has rendered the preceding clause vague, and has left room for theologians to interpret it in the milder sense of directive power.[10]

It is to be noted that Boniface VIII immediately added a statement justifying his action because of the superiority of the judicial power of the Church. He stated: "The spiritual power has to direct (*instituere*) the civil power, and to judge it if it is not good. Thus the prophecy of Jeremiah is verified concerning the Church and the power of the Church, 'Behold this day I have constituted you over nations and kingdoms' . . . Therefore, if there is an abuse of civil power, it is to be judged by the spiritual power, . . . if of the supreme power, by God alone, according to the testimony of the Apostle: 'The spiritual man judges all; He, however, is judged by no one.' "

It is to be remembered, however, that even those who were strong advocates of papal power as applicable in civil affairs held that the temporal jurisdiction of the spiritual power was not to be exercised regularly and commonly,[11] and at this point the theory rested until the time of Bellarmine and Suarez.

The dispute between Boniface and Philip became bitter. Philip convened a group of barons and lawyers at the Louvre on June 13, 1303, charging the Pope with simony, heresy, and immorality of all

---

[10] Hergenröther, for instance, in commenting on this text, stated the possibility of translating this sentence as, "the spiritual power has to teach (*Instituere*) the civil power," and added: "If *'instituere'* is to be translated to appoint instead of to direct, at all events it can only apply to the anointing and crowning, and not to the elevation to the dignity; Boniface VIII expressly acknowledges *two powers ordained by God."—Catholic Church and Christian State,* Essay XI Part II, § 1 (Vol. II, 121).

[11] "Concludi potest quod spiritualis potestas temporalem jurisdictionem quam habet non debet exercere, immediate loquendo, regulariter et communiter."— Jacques de Viterbe, *De regimine Christiano,* I, 8, 10, fol. 92; edit. Perugi, (1301-1302), p. 148, as quoted by Rivière, *op. cit.,* p. 421. Concerning this work and the opinion of Jacques de Viterbe. Cf. Hull, *Medieval Theories of the Papacy and other Essays* (London: Burns Oates and Washbourne, 1934), pp. 36-47.

kinds. At daybreak of September 7, 1303, the infamous Nogaret and an armed mob stormed the papal chambers at Anagni, pulled the eighty-five year old Pope from his throne, and made him prisoner. He was rescued by the citizens three days later, and died of a fever October 11, 1303.

Even the death of Boniface did not assuage the hatred of Philip and Nogaret. The new Pope, Benedict XI (1303-1304) attempted to restore peace and order by quashing the anti-regal acts of Boniface, but he steadfastly refused to call a consistorial trial of the deceased Pope. Shortly after he published a Bull at Perugia demanding that those who participated in the attempt at Anagai appear before him, he died so suddenly as to cause a belief that he was poisoned.

For his efforts to preserve peace, Boniface was maligned and persecuted, but if the power of the medieval popes was to fall with him, it fell under a man who maintained great dignity and reserve, showing clemency, patience, and forgiveness to those who so sacrilegiously ill-treated him.[12]

The power of the Emperor had been destroyed with the deposition of Frederick II, and the temporal power of the Pope by Philip the Fair. The devisive spirit of nationalism replaced the common faith of Christendom. The ever increasing strength and development of the secular powers led them to feel that the supplementary functions of the Church were unnecessary, and even unjust restrictions and usurpations. The result was such events as that typified by the Conference of Vincennes, which was called by Philip VI (1328-1350) in 1329 to arbitrate the dispute regarding the scope of jurisdiction of the ecclesiastical courts against which the civil magistrates were complaining.[13]

B. *The Conflict in England*

The crucial battle was fought in England, and resulted not only in the loss of the temporal functions of the ecclesiastical courts, but in the rejection of the spiritual authority of the Church as well.

---

[12] Hergenröther, *Catholic Church and Christian State,* Essay XI (Vol. II, 98-143; *Mediaeval Political Theory,* V, chpts. 8, 9, 10, pp. 374-440; Hughes, *A History of the Church* (3 vols., New York: Sheed and Ward, 1934-1947), III, 56-86.

[13] Cf. Mansi, XXV, cols. 883-8.

None of this could be foreseen in the beginning. During the Anglo-Saxon period (between the landing of St. Augustine in 579 and the Battle of Hastings in 1066), the English made no distinction between the civil and the ecclesiastical courts. The bishops and sheriffs sat on the same bench to try both ecclesiastical and secular cases.[14]

The two courts were separated by an ordinance of William the Conqueror (1066-1087), in accordance with the canonical procedure on the Continent, which had been overlooked because of the remoteness of England from Rome and the undeveloped political nature of the times.[15]

The jurisdiction of the ecclesiastical courts grew extensively during the next hundred years, so much so, in fact, that Henry II (1154-1189) called a conference of civil and ecclesiastical magistrates at Clarendon in 1164 for the purpose of settling the dissension and discord which had arisen on this account through the dissatisfaction of the secular authorities.

The statutes which resulted from this conference provided: that controversies over advowsons between laymen and clerics were to be settled in the king's court (c. 1); that clerics accused of crime should be tried first in the king's court, then in the ecclesiastical court, and finally be sent back to the secular court for punishment (c. 2); that upon a second offense clerics were to be denied the right of protection by the Church (c. 3); that the defendant must be accused openly in the ecclesiastical court by the plaintiff, or, failing this, charges must be brought by the sheriff's jury (c. 6); that no tenant-in-chief should be excommunicated, nor his lands placed under interdict, unless the king first judged the secular aspects of the case (c. 7); that appeals in the ecclesiastical forum could be made as far as the court of the archbishop, but, beyond that, appeal lay only to the king's court (c. 8); that cases involving church property were to be tried by the secular courts unless they were held in free alms, but the secular courts were to determine this latter point (c. 9); that contempt of the

---

[14] Plucknett, *A Concise History of the Common Law* (Rochester, New York: Lawyers Co-operative Publishing Company, 1929), pp. 4-10 [hereafter cited *Common Law*]. Cf. Phillimore, "Jurisdiction," *A Dictionary of Christian Antiquities*, I, 894-8.

[15] Plucknett, *loc. cit.*

ecclesiastical court could be punished by interdict, but not by excommunication until after an investigation by the secular authority (c. 10); that lords were responsible to the king if their servants wronged a bishop (c. 13); that pleas of debt, though the debt was contracted under oath, were to be judged by the secular courts (c. 15).[16]

Thomas Becket, the Archbishop of Canterbury at the time (1162-1170), grudgingly assented to the statutes, but demurred when it came time to seal the documents which would have acknowledged the right of the temporal power to determine the objects and limits of ecclesiastical judicial power. Shortly afterwards he was convicted of contempt by Henry, and he fled into an exile which lasted for six years. Finally, returning to England, December 1, 1170, he was murdered before the month was out. Henry II was placed under an interdict, which was lifted two years later, with Henry conceding the right of jurisdiction in criminal cases involving clerics, and the right of appeal to Rome in ecclesiastical affairs, provided that there was no suspicion of disloyalty to the king, and that assurance was given that the appeal would not bring harm to king or kingdom.[17]

In 1215 Innocent III drove another wedge between the courts of Church and State by forbidding clerics to take part in trial by ordeal,[18] and, at the same time, paved the way for trial by jury by abolishing the one lawful means of trial known at the time.[19] The majority of judges, however, continued to be clerics until the time of Edward

---

16 Mansi, XXI, cols. 1187-1196; Plucknett, *op. cit.*, pp. 15-17.

17 *The Cambridge Medieval History*, 8 vols. (New York: Macmillan Co., 1911-1936), V, 557-566; Plucknett, *Common Law*, pp. 17-19.

18 *Decreta Generalia Concilii Laternensis IV*, Can. XVIII: "Sententiam sanguinis nullus clericus dictet aut proferat, sed nec sanguinis vindictam exerceat, aut ubi exercetur intersit. Si quis autem hujusmodi occasione statuti, ecclesiis vel personis ecclesiasticis aliquod praesumpserit inferre dispendium, per censuram ecclesiasticam compescatur. Nec quisquam clericus litteras scribat, aut dicta pro vindicta sanguinis destinandas. Unde in curiis principium haec solicitudo non clericis sed laicis committatur."—Harduin, *Acta Conciliorum et Epistolae Decretales ac Constitutiones Summorum Pontificum* (12 vols., Parisiis, 1714-1715), VII, cols. 54-55.

19 Plucknett, *op. cit.*, pp. 102-7.

20 *Ibid.*, p. 161.

II (1307-1327),[20] and the chancellors of the courts of Equity were clerics until the reign of Henry VIII (1509-1547).[21]

All recognition of the Church's right to judge marriage, divorce, perjury, usury, adultery, criminal cases involving clerics, defamation, and last wills and testaments was, of course, withdrawn at the time of the Protestant Reformation. The schismatic, national Church took over many of these functions, but lost the usurped jurisdiction, even over wills and marriages, in 1857.[22]

C. *Reformation Issues*

The dispute between Church and State at the time of the Reformation differed entirely, then, from the disputes at Vincennes and Clarendon.[23]

> Church and State had frequently quarreled during the Middle Ages, but it was the very intimacy which existed between them that provoked dissension. They were not two different powers, but merely two aspects of the one divine mission of ruling the souls and bodies of men by law. Law in the theological sense, and law as the lawyer knew it, were both based on the same foundation—the will of God as expressed through authority (whether ecclesiastical or royal), tradition and custom. To attack the authority of the Church was therefore to attack the whole mediaeval system of law.[24]

The legal revolt was aided by the anarchic principle of private interpretation of the Bible, which discarded fifteen hundred years of Christian traditions and custom, and was reflected in the legal sphere by a depreciation of custom and authority, which left the dictates of the State as the only source of law.[25] This was the origin of the "legal positivism" so prevalent among civil jurists today.

It was at this moment that two brilliant Jesuits entered the battle to defend the Church by clearly distinguishing between the temporal power of the pope and his power in temporalities, thus defining the limits and rights of the Church in temporal matters, the precise ex-

---

21 *Ibid.*, pp. 239-241.

22 Smith, *Handbook of Elementary Law*, p. 370.

23 Cf. *supra*, pp. 64-5.

24 Plucknett, *op. cit.*, p. 41.

25 *Ibid.*, p. 40.

tent of which had been the cause of so much controversy and dispute. They were Cardinal Robert Bellarmine (1542-1621) and Francisco Suarez (1548-1617).

Both Bellarmine, refuting the royal claims to spiritual power with biblical, historical, and philosophic arguments, in an exchange of pamphlets with James I (1603-1625),[26] and Suarez, clarifying the position of the Church in his tract, *Defense of the Catholic and Apostolic Faith against the Errors of the Anglican Sect* (1613),[27] rejected the doctrine of those who held that the Pope has the fullest measure of temporal power by divine right.[28] They explained, in keeping with the common, more moderate, more acceptable tradition of the Church, as found in the decretal *Per venerabilem* of Innocent III, who claimed to use temporal jurisdiction *casualiter* (as occasion demanded),[29] and in the decretal *Novit* of Innocent IV, who said that the Pope was not to judge directly concerning fiefs, but only indirectly by reason of sin,[30] and in harmony with the *De Consideratione* of St. Bernard, who made allowances for incidental and urgent cases,[31] and in union with a host of Catholic theologians,[32] that

---

26 Bellarmine argued: "If the laity have authority in the Church they have it from themselves or from another; they have it not of themselves, for spiritual authority is not a natural right, but a divine, positive, and supernatural prerogative; they have it not from another, for Christ said to St. Peter in particular, 'Feed my sheep,' (John, 21:17), 'The Holy Ghost has placed you bishops, to rule the Church of God.' (*Acts,* 20:28)."—*Pro Juramento Fidelitatis,* quoted in Rager, *Political Philosophy of Blessed Cardinal Bellarmine* (Washington, D. C.: Catholic University of America, 1926). p. 124.

27 Cf. *supra,* pp. 37-39.

28 Suarez argued that a just title for such power could be found neither from the natural law, since the Christian States are not united politically, nor as the result of an election or a just war, since there is no such historic fact, and no temporal prince ever possessed supreme, universal jurisdiction (though the Pope possesses dominion over the kingdom of Rome by the Donation of Constantine), nor from Scripture, since all the texts referred to by those who hold this opinion are to be interpreted as applying properly to spiritual power only. Cf. *Defensio Fidei,* Lib. III, Cap. V, nn. 7-14.

29 Cf. *supra,* pp. 48, 57.

30 Cf. *supra,* footnote 31, p. 50.

31 Cf. *supra,* pp. 60-61; *infra,* p. 70.

32 Cf. footnote 4, *supra,* pp. 38-9.

the power which the Pope has over temporalities is, not direct, but indirect. By this they meant that the pontifical power is fundamentally and properly spiritual, with spiritual affairs as the proper object with which it is directly concerned; but indirectly with temporal matters, in so far as they are ordered to, or affect, the spiritual, as an inference and necessary consequence, providing a secondary object to be dealt with in emergency.[33]

Bellarmine illustrated this idea by saying that the art of government is different and distinct from the art of sculpture, oratory, astronomy, etc. These are not derived from one another in any

[33] Cf. Bellarminus, *De Potestate Papae in Rebus Temporalibus, adversus Gulielmum Barclaium,* Cap. V (*Opera Omnia,* Parisiis, 1870-1874), XII, 26; Suarez, *Defensio Fidei,* Lib. III, Cap. V, n. 15. Suarez explained his idea of indirect power in number 2 of the same chapter: "That subjection is called direct which is confined within the object and bounds of this civil power itself; and that is called indirect which is derived solely from a striving towards an end that is nobler, and pertains to a superior and more excellent authority. For true civil power in its essence serves directly no other end than the fit condition and temporal felicity of a human commonwealth during this temporal life; and consequently, such power itself is also called temporal. Thus civil power is said to be supreme in its own order, when the ultimate decision in that order and with respect to the end thereof is referred to the said power, within its own sphere, that is to say, within the whole community subject to it; so that all inferior magistrates possessing power in such a community or in a part thereof, are dependent upon such a supreme prince, whereas this supreme sovereign himself is subject to no superior, in regard to the said purpose of civil government. For temporal and civil felicity must of course be related to spiritual and eternal felicity; and therefore, it may happen that the very subject-matter of civil power will require, for the attainment of a spiritual good, such direction and government as would not appear to be demanded otherwise by reasons of a purely civil nature. Under such circumstances, even though the temporal prince and his power may not be directly subject, in regard to his own acts, to any other power within the same order and serving solely the same [civil] end, nevertheless it may become necessary for this prince to be directed, aided, or corrected in his own field of activity by a higher power that governs men in relation to a more excellent and an eternal end. In that case, the dependence in question is called indirect dependence, since such a superior power is concerned with temporal affairs, not in themselves nor for their own sake, but (as it were) indirectly, and often on account of some other factor."—for reproduction of original text and translation cf. Carnegie, *Selections.*

way, but are unique in their own spheres. Standards of the sculptor and orator are not established by the government, but nonetheless they remain subservient to good government. The governor might order the sculptor to refrain from producing obscene statues and pictures which would corrupt the morals of the people. He might demand that the sculptor use no bronze, gold, or silver, on the grounds that these were materials directly, or essentially, necessary to the government. Certainly no one would consider such restrictions placed by the ruler on the sculptor as undue or unreasonable interference. In the same manner, the higher and superior purposes to be attained by the Church give her a right, not by reason of any temporal power, but in view of her spiritual mission, to similar intervention. Therefore, if the matter in question should be one which would endanger the salvation of souls, the law of the emperor is abrogated by the law of the pontiff. When the matter is temporal in nature, and not concerned with the salvation of souls, the pontifical law does not abrogate the emperor's law, but both are to be upheld, the civil law in the civil courts, and the ecclesiastical law in the ecclesiastical courts.[34]

Furthermore, Suarez pointed out that temporal power does not belong to the Church in such a manner that, for its exercise, there must intervene a complete concession or delegation of that power to the civil authorities, for if this were done in such a way that the Church could no longer revoke, limit, correct or amend the acts of its delegates, such a possession would prove completely useless. On the other hand, the concession could not be made in such manner that there would remain the option of an arbitrary interference on the part of the spiritual power, for in such an event both hatred and envy could all too readily ensue.[35]

Again, the indirect power of the Church is not limited to a directive force, but involves real legislative, judicial, and punitive powers, for a purely directive force is ineffectual with reference to incorrigibly wicked temporal princes, as also with schismatics and stubborn heretics.[36]

---

[34] Bellarmine, *De Romano Pontifice,* Lib. V, Cap. VI (*Opera Omnia,* I, 531-2). Cf. Hull, *Medieval Theories of the Papacy and other Essays,* Capt., 1.

[35] Suarez, *Defensio Fidei,* Lib. III, Cap. V, nn. 20-1.

[36] Suarez, *ibid.,* Cap. XXIII.

Regarding the judicial power of the Church Bellarmine concluded:

> The pope, as pope, cannot ordinarily judge temporal affairs, for Bernard rightly says, 'Here below and on earth these have their own judges, the kings and princes of the land. Why invade the territory of others? Why extend your scythe into another's harvest?,' and again 'Your power is in criminal matters, not in civil arguments.' But, nonetheless, in a case in which it is necessary for the salvation of souls, the pontiff can preside even over temporal judicial trials. Certainly he can do this when there is no other who can judge, as when two kings contend, or when those who can and should judge, do not wish to render sentence. Therefore Bernard adds, 'but it is one thing to venture into these things incidentally, and quite another to apply oneself to them as being worthy of such, and with the intention of such.' Innocent III, in *per venerabilem, Qui Filii Sint Legitimi,* says that the pontiff exercises temporal jurisdiction only incidentally (*casualiter*)![37]
>
> This much is certain, and well recognized, that the Supreme Pontiff can for a just reason, such as the salvation of souls, the freedom of religion, or the conservation of the Church, judge in temporalities and even depose temporal princes.[38]

The efforts of Bellarmine and Suarez could not undo the religious anarchism, the unbridled nationalism, and the unlimited monarchism unleashed by the Reformation. Whereas the conflicts of the past had

---

[37] "Quantum ad judicia, non potest papa ut papa ordinarie judicare de rebus temporalibus: recte enim Bernardus Eugenio Lib. I, *De Consid.* dicit. 'Habent haec infima et terrena judices suos, reges et principes terrae. Quid fines alienos invaditis? Quid falcem vestram in alienam messem extenditis?' Item: 'In criminibus, non in possessionibus, potestas vestra.' At nihilominus, in casu quo id animarum saluti necessarium est, potest pontifex assumere etiam temporalia judicia, quando nimirum non est ullus qui possit judicare, ut cum duo reges supremi contendunt, vel quando qui possunt, et debent judicare, non volunt sententiam ferre. Unde ibidem Bernardus: 'sed aliud est,' inquit, 'incidenter excurrere in ista, aliud vero incumbere istis, tamquam dignis tali, et talium intentione rebus.' Et Innocentius III, cap. *Per Venerabilem, qui fil. sint legit.,* dicit jurisdictionem temporalem solum casualiter pontificem exercere."—*De Romano Pontifice,* Lib. V, Cap. VI (*Opera Omnia,* I, 532).

[38] Bellarmine, *De Potestate Papae in Rebus Temporalibus,* Cap. III (*Opera Omnia,* XII, 20). Concerning the deposition of princes cf. Cappello, *Summa Iuris Publici Ecclesiastici,* n. 232; Suarez, *Defensio Fidei,* Lib. III, Cap. XXIII; Ottaviani, *Institutiones Juris Publici Ecclesiastici,* II, n. 316.

revolved about the activity of the Church in the temporal sphere, now its very spiritual authority over matters which were exclusively the Church's own was called into question and invaded.

D. *Post-Reformation Regalism*

This invasion of the spiritual sphere by the temporal power was the inevitable result of the rejection of the spiritual authority of the Church by the Protestants. In denying that the Church of Rome was the true Church of Christ the Reformers were forced to separate religion from the Church, and to maintain that Christianity was an invisible society, or at most a fraternal union of those who held common beliefs and maintained a fellowship of hope and charity.[39]

To replace the divinely constituted, living, social authority by which positive dogmas and morals had been transmitted and conserved throughout fifteen hundred years, the Reformers substituted individual inspiration in the interpretation of the Bible, though to do this they had to deny that the Church's existence antedated the completed Bible by two generations. The immediate result of this was the deprivation of any logical basis, or hope, upon which they could claim for themselves any spiritual authority, for if religion is a matter of immediate revelation and personal experience, then all are equal in such a way that each is free to think on every subject just as he may choose, and to do whatever he may like to do, so that each one is his own master and no man has any right to rule over other men.[40]

Religion, then, being entirely a spiritual and personal matter, had to be considered by the Reformers as little more than a personal philosophy of life. The denial of the authority of the Church as established by a positive act of God forced them to hold that, if any religious societies exist, they are but the voluntary banding together of those who have similar experiences. They are, therefore, not

39 "By the Church, said Luther, I understand the society of all those who live in faith, in hope, and in charity. Thus the essence, the life, and the nature of Christianity do not consist in a corporal assembly, but in the unions of hearts in a common faith."—Quoted by Moulart, *L'Eglise et l'Etat* (Louvain, Paris, 1887), p. 21.

40 Cf. Leo XIII, ep. encycl. *Immortale Dei—Fontes,* n. 592; Cappello, *Summa Iuris Publici Ecclesiastici,* nos. 131, 139. Cf. Moulart, *op. cit.,* p. 26.

divine, but merely naturally emergent factors in the spiritual field of man's gregarious nature.[41]

Since they had rejected the Church, and could not logically claim to possess spiritual authority of themselves in a society which was founded on individualism and the very denial of authority, the Reformers had to look to the State for this purpose. Three major solutions were offered. According to Matthias Stephani (c. 1570-1646), the bishops had legitimate authority until the religious peace of Augsburg in 1555, at which time their power was suspended and devolved upon the secular princes. Hugo Grotius (1583-1645), and Mozer proffered the opinion that the secular prince exercises proper jurisdiction over all things of whatever kind within his territory, and that since the Church exists within the territory of civil rulers, the prince has proper authority over the Church. Accordingly, they modified the first opinion by teaching that the Peace of Augsburg did not cause the spiritual authority to devolve upon the prince, but rather restored what was his by native and proper right. A more satisfactory basis for the Protestant system of churches was offered by Samuel von Puffendorf (1632-1694) and Christopher Pfaff (1686-1760) and popularized by Justus Henning Boehmer (1674-1749). They held that just as the citizens have a natural right to form associations, colleges and corporations for purposes of business, education, and fraternity, so they have a natural right to form associations for religious purposes. As in all other imperfect, voluntary societies, all members are equal, there being no real jurisdiction, but only a dominative power according to the freely conceded, contractual agreement of the members. It draws its civil rights from a state charter, and the civil powers oversee its activities, enforce its contractual by-laws, and protect both the society and its members from injury and interference.

The right which the State acquires over religious affairs through such a system is held to be indirect, for though religion does not directly pertain to the object of the State, nevertheless the religious activity of its citizens seriously affects the peace and order of society at large. A twofold right and duty of the State is recognized under this system. First it has a negative duty of surveillance in order

[41] Moulart, *L'Eglise et l'Etat*, pp. 20-27.

to prevent crimes, frauds, deceptions, or any other nefarious actions from being perpetrated under the guise of religion.[42] Then it has a positive duty of aiding and protecting the Church which it has established, or at least licensed, so that the activity of the Church will be directed to the utility of the State and its citizens. The State, therefore, has the duty to regulate, judge, and protect, as the common, public welfare demands, the appointment of preachers, ecclesiastical ordinations, rites, the manner of teaching, sacred trials and religious controversies, ecclesiastical boundaries and the constitution of churches and the matter of public teaching.[43] These systems, evidently, postulated a total capitulation of the spiritual power to the State.[44]

The theory of regalism, i.e., that the civil authority possesses authority in spiritual matters, can be traced back to the fourteenth century to Marsilius of Padua (ca. 1343) and Jean de Jandun (fl. 1315-1328), who wrote a tract called the *Defensor Pacis,* in which society was considered to be a purely human institution, so that the spiritual power, i.e., the legislative, judicial, and punitive power of the Church, belonged to the nation of Christian people. The people transferred this power through the hands of the civil prince to the members of the spiritual hierarchy, who thus became responsible and subject to judgement and deposition by the prince, if he was a Catholic, and by the people, if he was not a Catholic.[45]

In his constitution, *Licet iuxta doctrinae,* of October 23, 1327, John XXII (1316-1334) condemned the propositions of Marsilius: that the paying of the tax by Christ to Caesar meant that all the temporali-

---

[42] "Haec libertas Ecclesiae tamen non impedit quominus imperans prospicere et praecavere possit, imo debeat, ne sub praetextu sacrorum, scelera fraudes, coniurationes, aliquae nefanda committantur."—Boehmer, *Introductio in Ius Publ. Univ.,* c. V, § 15 (Ottaviani, *Institutiones Juris Publici Ecclesiastici,* n. 299). Cf. Moulart, *ibid.,* pp. 28-30.

[43] Boehmer, *op. cit.,* c. V, §§ 17, 19, 21, 22, 23, 29, 24, 26, 27 (Ottaviani, *loc. cit.*). Cf. Stokes, *Church and State in the United States* (3 vols., New York: Harper & Brothers, 1950), I, 43-7.

[44] Cf. Moulart, *op. cit.,* pp. 26-30; Ottaviani, *op. cit.,* n. 299; Coronata, *Jus Publicum Ecclesiasticum,* n. 41.

[45] Cf. Cappello, *Summa Iuris Publici Ecclesiastici,* nos. 147-8; Coronata, *Ius Publicum Ecclesiasticum,* n. 41; Moulart, *L'Eglise et l'Etat,* pp. 30-1; Cambridge Summer School of Catholic Studies, 1935, *Church and State,* pp. 90-1; Hull, *Medieval Theories of the Papacy and Other Essays,* Chap. VII.

ties of the Church are subject to the emperor;[46] that Peter did not have any more authority than the other Apostles, and that Christ had commissioned no head of the Church, nor made anyone his vicar;[47] that it pertained to the emperor to correct, institute, depose, and punish the pope;[48] that all priests, be they pope, archbishop, or simple priest, are of the same authority and jurisdiction by the institution of Christ;[49] that the whole Church together cannot punish any man without the consent of the emperor.[50]

In the seventeenth century Edmond Richer (1560-1631) also taught that the ecclesiastical hierarchy was responsible to the people, since Christ had conferred the supreme authority of the Church upon the Church as a whole, rather than on Peter as an individual. Furthermore, according to Richer, since the Church had neither any territory nor the right of the sword from Christ, it can use only persuasion and direction in its employment of the means necessary for salvation, but not force or temporal penalties. It is rather the political prince, as Lord of the republic and the territory, who is the defender and protector of the natural and canonical divine law. Consequently for this purpose he can make laws and draw the sword. As protector of the Church and defender of its sacred canons, he is the legitimate judge of appeals from alleged abuse.[51]

Similar errors were found in the earlier works of Pierre Pithou (1539-1596), who was the first to systematize the system called Gallicanism.[52] He taught that the popes have no jurisdiction, general or particular, in anything pertaining to the temporal order, in the lands and possessions subject to a very Christian king, and that, though the pope may be recognized as sovereign in spiritual matters, his authority is nonetheless not absolute and unlimited in the Church

---

46 *Enchiridion Symbolorum et Declarationum de Rebus Fidei et Morum* (ed. Denzinger, Bannwart, Umberg 21-23 ed., Friburgi Brisgoviae: Herder Co., 1937), n. 495 (hereafter cited Denzinger).

47 Denzinger, n. 496.

48 Denzinger, n. 497.

49 Denzinger, n. 499.

50 Denzinger, n. 500.

51 Richer, *De Ecclesiastica et Politica Potestate,* Cap. 10-13, cited in Moulart, *op. cit.,* p. 33; Cappello, *op. cit.,* n. 153.

52 Cf. *infra,* pp. 75-76.

of France, but tempered and limited by the canons and regulations of the ancient councils of the Church received in France.[53]

In 1763 Nikolaus von Hontheim (1701-1790) under the name of Justinus Febronius, published a book called *De Statu Ecclesiae* in which he taught that the primacy of the pope derived, not from divine law, but from the *placitum* of the Church, so that his authority was of a directive rather than a coercive nature. The individual bishops received the power of jurisdiction as well as the power of orders directly from God, and consequently their power over ecclesiastical discipline was full and absolute. The civil princes were the guardians and protectors of the ecclesiastical canons, and had the right to hear appeals from abuse when made against the Church, especially against the decisions of the Roman Pontiff.[54]

These false doctrines were also reflected in the works of Charles Fevret (1583-1661), Pierre de Marca (1594-1662), Jean Launcy (1603-1678), Pierre Dupuy (1582-1651), Etienne Baluze (1630-1718), Pasquier Quesnel (1634-1719), Louis Dupin (1657-1719), Jacques Bossuet (1627-1704),[55] and their theories were, under different names, applied to the actual restriction of the rights of the Church in various countries. In Germany it was called Caesarism; in France, Gallicanism; in Austria, Josephinism; in Italy, Jurisdictionalism.

Gallicanism reached its apex in France with the Declaration of the Four Articles by the Assembly of the Clergy of France convoked on March 19, 1682, by Louis XIV (1643-1715). These four articles declared: 1) that the jurisdiction of the pope was limited to spiritual things and those which concern salvation, but did not extend to civil and temporal matters; 2) that the oecumenical councils are superior to the pope; 3) that the pope is subject to the common law in the

---

[53] Pithou, *Nouveaux Opuscules,* p. 171, cited in Moulart, *op. cit.,* p. 35; cf. Cappello, *op. cit.,* n. 151.

[54] Cf. Cappello, *op. cit.,* n. 155; Coronata, *Ius Publicum Ecclesiasticum,* n. 41.

[55] Cf. Cappello, *Summa Iuris Publici Ecclesiastici,* n. 152; the condemnation of Jansenism, Pius VI, const. *Auctorem Fidei,* Aug. 28, 1794—*Fontes,* n. 475; props. 2, 3, 4, 5, 6, 78, 59, 60, etc.; Van Hove, *Prolegomena ad Codicem Iuris Canonici* (2. ed., Mechliniae Romae: H. Dessain, 1945), n. 518.

exercise of his authority, and 4) that the pope has indeed the principal function to play in questions of faith, but that his decisions are not immutable until after their acceptance and consent by the universal Church.[56]

Josephinism in Austria (1780-1855) took its name from Joseph II (1765-1790), who accepted the teachings of "Febronius" and added the principle of regal absolutism and territorial plenitude of power, so that, in effect, the Church became merely an instrument of the State.[57]

Jurisdictionalism originated with the Peace of Westphalia (1648). It flourished in some German States, in France, in Holland, and in Italy, and ceased with the treaty between Italy and the Holy See in 1929. It differed from the Regalism which chartered and governed an exclusive, established Church, in that it recognized and tolerated several churches, regulating and sometimes subsidizing them on an equal level.[58]

---

[56] The first Article, which pertains most properly to the relation of Church and State, declares: "We have judged it fitting to declare: 1. that God has given to Saint Peter and to his successors, the vicars of Jesus Christ, and to the Church itself, power over spiritual things and those which concern eternal salvation, but not over civil and temporal things, for the Lord has said, 'My kingdom is not of this world,' and in another place, 'Render then to Caesar the things that are Caesar's,' and that thus this precept of the Apostle remains sound, 'let every person be subject to superior powers, for there is no power which does not come from God, and those which exist are ordained by God. Therefore he who resists authority resists the order of God.' We declare, consequently, that the kings and sovereigns are not subject to any ecclesiastical authority in temporal things by the order of God; that by the authority of the keys of the Church the sovereigns cannot be deposed either directly or indirectly, or their subjects dispensed from the fidelity, the obedience, and the obligation of the oaths of fidelity to which they have sworn; and that this doctrine, which is necessary to the public tranquillity, and no less advantageous to the Church than to the State, must be inviolably followed as conforming to the word of God, the tradition of the Fathers, and the examples of the saints."—cited in Moulart, *L'Eglise et l'Etat,* pp. 36-7. Cf. also, *ibid., pp.* 34-39; 47-8; Cappello, *op. cit.,* n. 150.

[57] Cf. Cappello, *op. cit.,* n. 156; Ottaviani, *Institutiones Iuris Publici Ecclesiastici,* n. 229.

[58] Cf. Stokes, *Church and State in the United States,* I, 45-7.

It seemed to Pius IX (1846-1878) that all the pent-up fury of the Reformation had matured to burst upon his pontificate.[59] Not a single European country was on avowedly friendly terms with the Church. The forces of a uniting Italy had driven him in flight to Gaëta in 1848, and he ended his days as a voluntary prisoner of the Vatican in protest against the despoliation of the Vatican Domains.[60]

While Napoleon III (1852-1870) had kept troops in Rome to protect the interests of the Pope until 1870, the "Ultramontanists" were just beginning to make headway against the Gallican movement in France itself. The French civil courts still claimed the right to hear appeals on such ecclesiastical matters as the reservation of benefices to the Roman Curia, and sentences *ex informata conscientia,* while among the Organic Articles, which were added later to the Napoleonic Concordat, was the provision that recourse was to be had to the State Authority in all cases of abuse on the part of superiors and other ecclesiastical persons. The cases of abuse were listed as: usurpation or exceeding of power, transgression of the laws and regulations of the Republic, infraction of the rules consecrated by the canons received in France, attempts against the liberties, franchises, and customs of the Church of France, and every undertaking, or every procedure, that, in the exercise of worship, could compromise the honor of its citizens, arbitrarily trouble their conscience, or engender any oppression, injury, or public scandal against them.[61]

Caesarism was prevalent in Switzerland, the Grand Duchies of Baden and Hesse, and in the kingdoms of Saxony and Prussia, where the schism of the "Old Catholics" and persecution developed over the definition of papal infallibility (1870). A concordat was negotiated for Spain in 1851, but was soon rendered ineffective by political revolutions there, while in Portugal the Church was controlled by the State, whose officials forbade the bishops to visit Rome in 1860. Italy was at odds with Austria soon after the election of Pius, and

59 Allocut. *Multis gravibusque,* Dec. 17, 1860—*Fontes,* n. 529.

60 Cf. Allocut. *Iamdudum cernimus,* March 18, 1861—*Fontes,* n. 530; Allocut. *Maxima quidem,* June 9, 1862, *Fontes,* n. 534; Seppelt-Löffler, *A Short History of the Popes* (adapted from the German by Preuss, St. Louis, Mo.: B. Herder Co., 1932), pp. 421-461.

61 Cf. Ottaviani, *Institutiones Iuris Publici Ecclesiastici,* II, n. 353.

his refusal to become involved cost him his popularity at home, but the last remnants of Josephinism were erased by means of a concordat with Franz Joseph (1848-1916) in 1855. The governments of South America were running rough shod over the rights of the Church, particularly in Columbia,[62] and in Mexico, where open persecution had broken out.[63]

It is little wonder, then, that Pius IX found it necessary to complain bitterly, and to denounce the rationalists and modernists, who wished to replace faith with reason,[64] holding that revelation was not only useless but even harmful and imperfect, inasmuch as it obstructed progress; and to repudiate the so-called progress of these same modern sophisticates, whose pride in their own powers of reasoning had advanced them to the belief that even Our Lord Jesus Christ is but a myth and a fiction, that laws do not receive their obligating force from God, that, indeed, no such a thing as divine law exists,[65] and who would not be satisfied until every principle of authority, every restraint of religion, and every rule of right and justice would be destroyed.[66]

On December 8, 1864, the Holy Father published his encyclical *Quanta cura,*[67] along with a *Syllabus Errorum,*[68] listing eighty errors which he had previously condemned. As a result of the flood of doctrinal and physical attacks made upon the liberties and rights of the Church he found it necessary to condemn the following propositions: The Church is not a juridically perfect and fully free society, nor does it enjoy any proper and constant rights as bestowed upon it by its divine Founder, but the civil power is to decide what are the rights and limits within which these same rights can be exercised (19); the status of the Republic, as the origin and source of all rights, enjoys a right which is bound by no limits (39); the ecclesiastical power cannot exercise its authority without the permission

62 Allocut. *Acerbissimum,* Sept. 27, 1852—*Fontes,* n. 515.

63 Allocut. *Nunquam fore,* Dec. 15, 1856—*Fontes,* n. 522.

64 Ep. encycl. *Singulari quidem,* March 17, 1856—*Fontes,* n. 521; *Syllabus Errorum,* 1864, §§ I, II—*Fontes,* n. 543.

65 Allocut. *Maxima quidem,* June 9, 1862—*Fontes,* n. 534.

66 Allocut. *Iamdudum cernimus,* March 18, 1861—*Fontes,* n. 530.

67 *Fontes,* n. 542.

68 *Fontes,* n. 543.

and consent of the civil government (20); kings and princes are not only exempt from the jurisdiction of the Church, but, indeed, in questions of jurisdiction they are superior (54); in conflicts between the laws of the two societies, the civil law prevails (42); the sacred ministers of the Church and the Roman Pontiff are to be altogether excluded from every care and dominion of temporal things (27); bishops have no right to promulgate their apostolic letters without the permission of the government (28); the Church does not have a native and legitimate right to acquire and hold possessions (26); the civil power can concern itself with things which pertain to religion, morals, and spiritual administration, and hence it can render judgment concerning the instructions which the pastors of the Church issue as norms for consciences, and can also judge concerning the administration of the divine sacraments and the dispositions necessary to receive them (44); national Churches can be instituted which are fully withdrawn and severed from the authority of the Roman Pontiff (37); matrimonial and betrothal promises pertain by their nature to the civil forum (74); the ecclesiastical forum for the temporal causes of clerics, whether civil or criminal, is to be done away with all together, even without notification of, or against the protests of, the Apostolic See (31); to the civil power belongs the right of appeal from so-called abuses.

The protests of the Church, however, went unheeded for the most part. The Age of Secularism had matured, and the authority of the Church again stood unrecognized. The totalitarian states which emerged from the atheism, rationalism, naturalism, and philosophical, political and economic factors of those days would brand religion as "the opium of the People," and accordingly would try to crush it as an enemy of the State.

E. *Development of the Natural Law Theory*

Faced with a multitude of discordant sects, the modern nontotalitarian State adopted a *laissez-faire* policy of liberty and toleration. Occasioned by political necessity, this policy found its philosophical justification in the observation of religion from the purely natural law stand point. It was noted that the exercise of religion, as the justly due acknowledgment and fulfillment by man of his relationship and obligation towards God, is one of those legitimate, ennobling, universal inclinations and functions embedded by God in the very nature of man, and that the worship of the Creator, and the teaching and practice of morality are not only helpful, but essential to the good order and law respecting demeanor of the citizens of a State. From this it was concluded that the exercise of religion is an inalienable, civil right to be recognized by the State, not as a creation thereof, but as a pre-existing right of man, which the State can only respect and guarantee.

The government, therefore, had placed the basis for spiritual rights on the same natural level as had Boehmer,[69] but it advanced a step further. Boehmer had concluded that religious societies were a corollary to the civil right of religion, and that they were therefore voluntary societies to be chartered and regulated, or established by the State. The modern State likewise concluded that religious socities are voluntary, similar to business corporations or colleges, but the framers of the new constitution refused, and were, indeed, unable to select and establish a Church either from those already established in different Colonies, or even to establish several acceptable churches according to the system of Jurisdictionalism.[70] Instead of this it relegated all religions to the realm of private interests, and abdicated and denied all positive duties and rights in the spiritual sphere, ruling that the State "shall make no law respecting an establishment of religion, or prohibiting the free exercise thereof." [71]

The new system of non-establishment, or separation, offered several important improvements over the Regalism which had preceeded it. The State no longer claimed to be the source of religious rights and authority. The objectionable interference of the State in purely spiritual matters was eliminated. This system provided for that political, civil, and social tolerance and freedom of conscience which the ever increasing frequency of contacts between various religious confessions within the same country necessitated, and "which is, under these circumstances, a moral obligation even for

---

69 Cf. supra, pp. 72-3.

70 Cf. supra, p. 76.

71 *The Constitution of the United States of America,* First Amendment.

Catholics." [72] Indeed, in nations where the commingling of Catholic and non-Catholic citizens make it impractical to recognize the divine authority of the Church as such, the Church recognizes the legitimacy and merit of this system, for though it is thought that the Church would flourish more profitably with the patronage of the public power, and though the State and nation are morally bound to recognize the spiritual authority of the Church as bestowed upon it by its Divine Founder,[73] still the Church has no wish, or intention, to force an unwilling acceptance of its spiritual authority on an unwilling nation, even as it is unwilling to force such an acceptance on unwilling individuals.[74]

But having guaranteed "non-establishment" and the "free exercise" of religion, the State found that even freedom of religion could not be guaranteed as an absolute, unrestricted right. In the absence of a recognized and truly divine authority to insure religious discipline and respect for the natural, ecclesiastical, and civil law, there

---

[72] Pius XII, Allocution to the Sacred Roman Rota, Oct. 6, 1946—*AAS,* XXXVIII (1946), 393, Bouscaren, *op. cit.,* p. 255. Cf. also Powers, *Religious Liberty and the Police Power of the State,* Faculty of the School of Law of the Catholic University of America (Washington, D. C.: The Catholic University of America Press, 1948), p. 50.

[73] "Hoc enim ecclesiae apud vos [Episcopos Americanos] concessum est, non repugnante temperatione civitatis, ut nullis legum praepedita vinculis, contra vim defensa iure communi iustitiaque iudiciorum, tutam obtineat vivendi agendique sine offensione facultatem. Sed quamquam haec vera sunt, tamen error tollendus, ne quis hinc sequi existimet, petendum ab America exemplum optimi ecclesiae status: aut universe licere vel expedire, rei civilis reique sacrae distractas esse dissociatasque, more americano, rationes. Quod enim incolumis apud vos res est catholica, quod prosperis etiam auctibus crescit, id omnino fecunditati tribuendum, qua divinitus pollet ecclesia, quaeque si nullus adversetur, si nulla res impedimento sit, se sponte effert atque effundit; longe tamen uberiores editura fructus, si, praeter libertatem, gratia legum fruatur patrocinioque publicae potestatis." —Leo XIII, encycl. *Longinqua oceani,* Jan. 6, 1895, § 6—*Fontes,* n. 628. Cf. Fenton, "Principles Underlying Traditional Church-State Doctrine," *The American Ecclesiastical Review* [later *The Ecclesiastical Review*] (Philadelphia, 1899—), CXXVI (June 1952), pp. 452-62; cf. also May 1953.

[74] "Ad amplexandam fidem catholicam, nemo invitus cogatur."—can. 1351. Cf. Vermeersch-Creusen, *Epitome Juris Canonici,* (3 vols., Mechliniae-Romae: H. Dessain, Vol. I, 7 ed., 1949; Vol. II, 6 ed., 1940; Vol. III, 6 ed., 1946), I, nos. 4, 5, 6, 18.

is real danger of the perpetration of hoaxes and frauds in the name of religion, while the misguided and sometimes deluded "personal inspiration" of well intentioned religious fanatics, can be harmful to the public welfare, and in actual violation of even the natural, moral law of reason and common sense. Indeed the acceptance of an unlimited right to plead religious conviction as a defense for any and every act could lead to a practical nullification of all civil law.[75]

The State, therefore, necessarily assumed the negative duties outlined by Boehmer, and maintained a police power over religious matters. Inevitably, then, the theory of separation twists the theory of Suarez and Bellarmine so that the indirect power which they attributed to the Church now becomes the prerogative of the State. It is the State rather than the Church which is the absolute and final guardian and interpreter of the moral law. It is the peace and order of the civil society rather than morality and the welfare of the soul which is the supreme standard to be met. Admittedly, it is here, in these isolated, rare instances of conflicting spiritual and temporal interests, where the concord between both societies is disturbed, and where the claim to ultimate and absolute authority is at issue, that this system finds its most serious handicap. While the exercise of a police power over all moral questions is quite legitimate, and even necessary, when exercised over "natural," voluntary religious societies, it fails before the factual, divine institution of universal, spiritual authority factually bestowed upon Peter and the Apostles by Jesus Christ.

The State, however has little to fear from the claim of the Church to supreme authority over "moral" and "spiritual matters," and the Church, in turn, has little to fear, in practice, from the exercise of such a police power when exercised by a State which truly respects the natural law and the rights of conscience, since its own religious and moral principles are in the highest conformity with the natural

[75] "While Congress was deprived of all legislative power over mere opinion, it was left free to reach actions 'in violation of social duties or subversive of good order.' To hold otherwise, said the Court, would, 'be to make the preferred doctrine of religious belief superior to the law of the land and in effect to permit every citizen to become a law unto himself.' "—Powers, *op. cit.,* p. 44, treating of the *Reynolds v. United States* case (98 U.S. 145 (1878)), concerning polygamy before the Supreme Court.

law of reason, since it teaches devotion and obedience to one's country as a virtue, and since its policy of adapting itself to the law of the land in all material things, such as laws of contract,[76] reduces any conflict of civil and religious laws and interests to a minimum.

Applied to the judicial rights of the Church, this system of separation resembles the political policy of the ancient Romans who were unwilling to become involved in the religious squabbles of their Jewish subjects.[77] Again the ecclesiastical judiciary is considered by the State as "analogous in its character to standing arbitrators" [78] whose rights rest, according to the dominant judicial view, only on the natural, voluntary, contractual agreement of its members to conform to the regulations and authority of the society.[79] But even though the true jurisdictional nature of the judicial authority is thus unrecognized, the Courts have ruled that:

> The rule of action which should govern the civil courts, founded in a broad and sound view of the relations of church and state under our system of laws, and supported by the preponderating weight of judicial authority is, that, whenever the questions of discipline, or of faith, or ecclesiastical rule, custom, or law have been decided by the highest of these church judicatories to which the matter has been carried, the legal tribunals must accept such decisions as final, and as binding on them, in their application to the case before them.[80]

still these judicatories are so subordinated to the State as to cease, even in spiritual matters, whenever the State considers a serious and proximate threat of the welfare of the State is present.[81] Thus the

---

[76] Cf. can. 1529.

[77] Cf. *supra,* pp. 23-5.

[78] *Everett v. First Presbyterian Church.* 53, N.J. Eq., 500, 507; 32 Atl. 747; cf. Zollmann, *American Civil Church Law,* Faculty of Political Science of Columbia University, Vol. 77 (New York: Longmans, Green & Co., 1917), pp. 198-236.

[79] Cf. Torpey, *Judicial Doctrines of Religious Rights in America* (Chapel Hill: The University of North Carolina Press, 1948), p. 146.

[80] *Watson v. Jones,* 13 Wall. 679, 725; 20 L. Ed. 666,675 (1871). Cf. Torpey, *Judicial Doctrines of Religious Rights in America,* pp. 118-47.

[81] "A religious activity is beyond the limit of judicial protection only when it creates a substantial danger which is extremely serious and the imminence of which is extremely high, and when that danger can not be avoided by

system of separation presents a mixed blessing for the Church, for while denying, or at least being unable to recognize, the true, divine, authority of the Church, the "secular courts . . . claim . . . no jurisdiction over religious controversies, and will not question any decision of a church tribunal relating to its internal affairs, in the absence of an interference with civil or property rights." [82]

The cycle from a pagan to a neo-pagan world was thus completed, and the nature and function of the judicial power of the Church had become tested and tried, examined and clarified, under periods of persecution and establishment of faith and of secularism.

---

some other method which will leave religious freedom unrestained."—Summers, *The Sources and Limits of Religious Freedom,* 41 Ill. L. Rev. 53 (1946), quoted by Powers, *op. cit.,* p. 141. "To justify the overriding of religious scruples, however, there must be a clear justification thereof in the necessities of national or community life. Like the right of free speech, it is not to be overborne by the police power, unless its exercise presents a clear and present danger to the community."—*Barnette v. West Virginia State Board of Education,* 47, F. Supp. (D.C., W. Va.) 251 (1942). Cf. Powers, *op. cit.,* pp. 137-160.

[82] Torpey, *op. cit.,* p. 118; cf. also Stokes, *Church and State in the United States,* III, 369-403.

PART II—LEGISLATION OF THE PRESENT DAY: CANON 1553, § 1

CHAPTER V

THE PROPER AND EXCLUSIVE NATURE OF THE JUDICIAL POWER OF THE CHURCH

A. *Legislation*

It now remained only to give definitive expression to the principles concerning the judicial power of the Church. This the Church has done in Canon 1553, § 1 of the *Code of Canon Law*:

> § 1. The Church has the proper and exclusive right of judging:
>
> 1°. cases which relate to spiritual matters, and to matters annexed to the spiritual;
>
> 2°. violations of ecclesiastical laws, and all other acts in which sin is involved, in so far as the decision of the guilt and the infliction of ecclesiastical penalties are concerned;
>
> 3°. all civil and criminal cases of persons who enjoy the privilege of the ecclesiastical forum, as prescribed by canons 120, 614, and 680.[1]

B. *Explanation of Terms*

Basic to any determination of the objects and limits of the judicial power of the Church is a clear understanding of the nature of this power. Consequently the Church begins this determinative canon with the statement that its judicial power over certain objects is "proper and exclusive."

Judicial power is proper, or inherent, to the Church in origin and in nature: in origin, because it is directly received from God, and exists as a property of its status as a juridically perfect society; in nature or function, i.e., in its objects and limits, because these are

---

[1] Canon 1553—§ 1. Ecclesia iure proprio et exclusivo cognoscit: 1°. De causis quae respiciunt res spirituales et spiritualibus adnexas; 2°. De violatione legum ecclesiasticarum deque omnibus in quibus inest ratio peccati, quod attinet ad culpae definitionem et poenarum ecclesiasticarum irrogationem; 3°. De omnibus causis sive contentiosis sive criminalibus quae respiciunt personas privilegio fori gaudentes ad normam can. 120, 614, 680.

identical with those of the Church: to secure the heavenly and eternal values.[2]

From this characteristic of properness there immediately flows the attribute of exclusiveness, or independence, which is the negative expression of its self-containment and inherence in the origin and nature of the Church. It expresses the connotation that the judicial power of the Church does not have its origin in any free, contractual consent of its members, nor in any delegation of the civil society, and does not find itself absorbed or contained within the nature and scope of any other power. The judicial power of the Church is exclusive, therefore, because it does not depend in the slightest degree upon any human power for its existence or object, and consequently is not subject to any permissive decree, interference, or surveillance from any outside power.[3]

C. *Foundation for these Characteristics*

So fundamental are these characteristics to the right understanding of the judicial function of the Church that recent Roman Pontiffs, especially Leo XIII and Pius XII, have carefully noted how they are rooted in the very origin and nature of the Church as a perfectly self-contained society.

1. The Church is a juridically perfect society

The juridic status of the Church had become clarified during the tradition-laden centuries. It was definitively ascertained to be "a society chartered as of right divine, perfect in its nature and in its title to possess in itself and by itself, through the will and loving kindness of its Founder, all needful provision for its maintenance." [4]

---

[2] Pius XII, Allocution to the Sacred Roman Rota, Oct. 29, 1947—*AAS,* XXXIX (1947), 494-5; Bouscaren, *The Canon Law Digest,* Supplement through 1948, pp. 216, 218.

[3] While the judicial power of the Church is a proper and exclusive function of the ecclesiastical government, not all matters pertain to its jurisdiction in a manner both proper and exclusive. The Church's jurisdiction over a particular object may be proper apart from being also exclusive, the State, at times sharing a proper and cumulative power with the Church, as will be explained below.

[4] Leo XIII, ep. encycl. *Immortale Dei—Fontes,* n. 592; *The Catholic Mind,* Nov. 8, 1936, p. 430.

The Church is a juridically perfect society,[5] i.e., self-sufficient and independent in its purposes and means,[6] for the Church is unique among the societies of the world. Its purpose, the salvation of souls, is spiritual, and therefore escapes the temporal limits which bind and subject all other societies to the State, whose object is the general, temporal welfare of mankind. Indeed, in so far as the spiritual purposes of life are above the temporal, being more essential, more sacred, and more permanent to man, the Church is elevated to a superior plane above the State in point of finality.[7] Moreover, the Church possesses all the means, and, therefore, all the social authority,[8] necessary and useful to its purposes, for, since the Church was instituted by divine decree, which decree emanated not only from the divine Will, but from the divine Wisdom as well, it is absurd to think that it was not given adequate means simultaneously with its supreme mission. This is especially so if one but consider that, were the Church to draw its authority and means from temporal societies, the superior and more essential society would be subordinated to the inferior, and its freedom, unity, and universality, would thereby be destroyed, for there would be as many churches, and as many rulers, as donors of authority.[9] Therefore, as a juridic society, founded as a necessary means of salvation for all men by positive divine law,[10] its means, and authority, are not based merely upon the free, contractual consent of its members, as are those of the voluntary societies within the State. As a spiritual society, its means, and consequently its authority, are proportionately spiritual and supernatural, and so beyond the power of the temporal power to supply. The Church, then, is juridically a perfect society, striving for the supreme and ultimate

[5] The Church is commonly defined by Catholic theologians as "coetus hominum viatorum eiusdem fidei christianae professione et eorundem sacramentorum participatione adunatus sub regimine legitimorum pastorum ac praecipue Romani Pontificis."—Tanquerey, *Synopsis Theologiae Dogmaticae* (24. ed., Parisiis: Typis Societatis Sancti Joannis Evangelistae, 1938), I, n. 543; Cf. Cappello, *Summa Iuris Publici Ecclesiastici,* nos. 91-102.

[6] Cf. *supra,* pp. 9-10, 13.

[7] Cappello, *op. cit.,* nos. 105; 113.

[8] As a part is contained in the whole. Cf. *supra,* pp. 4-5.

[9] Coronata, *Ius Publicum Ecclesiasticum,* nos. 42, 43; Cappello, *op. cit.,* nos. 105, 107, 109, 122, 137.

[10] Cf. *supra,* p. 13.

goal of the spiritual life, and possessing, in and of itself, all the means and authority necessary for the accomplishment of its purposes, by a proper and an exclusive right.

It is this status of the Church as a juridically perfect society, with its innate title to all the means necessary and useful for the accomplishment of its mission, that is the keystone to the determination of the rights and authority of the Church, and hence to the possession of a proper and exclusive judicial power.[11]

2. The Church possesses a judicial power proper and exclusive to itself, because its origins are found in the expressed will of its divine Founder.[12]

> The judicial power is an essential part and a necessary function of the two perfect societies, the Church and the State.[13] Hence the question of the origin of judicial power in each is the same as that of the origin of their authority in general.[14]
>
> Therefore, though all public power must proceed from God . . . and . . . everything without exception must be subject to Him, and must serve Him, so that whosoever holds the right to govern, holds it from one sole and single force, namely, the Sovereign Ruler of all, 'There is no power but from God,[15] . . . the fact is that the authority of the Church, and hence also its judicial power, are essentially different from those of the State . . . The origin of the Church, in contrast to that of the State, is not from the natural law. The most complete and accurate analysis of the human person offers no ground for the conclusions that the Church, like civil society, was naturally bound to come into existence and to develop. The Church is the product of a positive act of God, and is therefore on a plane above the social nature of man, though in perfect accord with it; and hence the authority of the Church—and

[11] Coronata, *op. cit.*, n. 21.

[12] Cf. *supra*, pp. 13-15, concerning the direct commission of judicial power to the Church.

[13] Cf. *supra*, pp. 1-5.

[14] Pius XII, Allocution to the Sacred Roman Rota, Oct. 2, 1945—*AAS*, XXXVII (1945), 257; Bouscaren, *The Canon Law Digest*, Supplement through 1948, p. 208.

[15] Leo XIII, ep. encycl. *Immortale Dei*—*Fontes*, n. 592, *The Catholic Mind*, Nov. 8, 1936, pp. 426-7.

> consequently her corresponding judicial power—are born of the will and act by which Christ founded His Church.[16]
>
> Hence, according to the Apostle the Holy Spirit calls Bishops to the office of judge no less than to the government of the Church. The sacred character of that office, therefore, comes from the Holy Spirit.[17]

The judicial power of the Church, then, is a right conferred upon the Church directly by God, and is entirely distinct in origin from that of the State, so that it need not, and cannot, in any way, be granted, delegated, or licensed by the State. In other words, since "for the Church the primary source of authority is the express will of Christ,"[18] its judicial power, which is an integral part of that authority, is, in its origins, proper and exclusive to the Church.

3. The Church possesses a judicial power proper and exclusive to itself because of the nature and object of the Church.

> It remains true, however, that once the Church was established as a perfect society by the act of the Redeemer, there sprang from her very nature not a few elements of resemblance to the structure of civil society.[19]
>
> A rapid and superficial survey of judicial laws and practice might give the impression that ecclesiastical and civil procedure present only secondary differences, about the same as those which are to be observed in the administration of justice in two States which belong to the same juridical family. They seem to coincide in their immediate purpose: the enforcement or protection, either through a judicial sentence or through an authoritative decree rendered according to law, of a right which is established by law but which is contested or violated in a particular case.[20]

---

[16] Pius XII, Allocution to the Sacred Roman Rota, Oct. 2, 1945—*AAS*, XXXVII (1945), 259; Bouscaren, *ibid.*, pp. 210-11.

[17] Pius XII, Allocution to the Sacred Roman Rota, Oct. 29, 1947—*AAS*, XXXIX (1947), 497; Bouscaren, *ibid.*, p. 218.

[18] Pius XII, Allocution to the Sacred Roman Rota, Oct. 2, 1945—*AAS*, XXXVII (1945), 261; Bouscaren, *ibid.*, p. 213.

[19] Pius XII, Allocution to the Sacred Roman Rota, Oct. 2, 1945—*AAS*, XXXVII (1945), 259; Bouscaren, *ibid.*, p. 211.

[20] Pius XII, Allocution to the Sacred Roman Rota, Oct. 2, 1945—*AAS*, XXXVII (1945), 256-7; Bouscaren, *ibid.*, p. 208.

> There is, however . . . that difference as regards the end, which has a profound and different influence on the Church and the State, especially on the supreme power of the two societies, and hence also on the judicial power, which is but one of their parts and functions.[21]
>
> The only-begotten Son of God established on earth a society which is called the Church . . . and it is the Church and not the State, that is to be man's guide to heaven. It is to the Church that God has assigned the charge of seeing to, and legislating for, all that concerns religion; of teaching all nations; of spreading the Christian faith as widely as possible; in short, of administering freely and without hindrance, in accordance with her own judgment, all matters that fall within her competence.[22]
>
> Whether, therefore, individual ecclesiastical judges are conscious of it or not, all their judicial activity is and remains within the scope of the full life of the Church, with her exalted end: *to secure the heavenly and eternal values.* This *finis operis* of the ecclesiastical judicial power impresses upon it an objective character and makes it an institution of the Church as a supernatural society. . . . Thus we are ever encountering anew the profound difference which the diversity of ends makes between the ecclesiastical and the civil judicial powers.[23]

Thus the Church and the State, each possessing within itself sufficient power to accomplish its end, and each with a separate and supreme purpose in its own order, the one having "for its proximate and chief objective the well-being of this mortal life; the other the everlasting joy of heaven," [24] are two proper and exclusive societies, perfect and distinct by reason of their ends, as well as their origins, as also are the judicial powers which each possesses.

---

[21] Pius XII, Allocution to the Sacred Roman Rota, Oct. 29, 1947—*AAS,* XXXIX (1947), 495; Bouscaren, *ibid.,* p. 216. Cf. also Marchesi, *Summula Iuris Publici Ecclesiastici,* n. 10.

[22] Leo XIII, ep. encycl. *Immortale Dei—Fontes,* n. 592; *The Catholic Mind,* Nov. 8, 1936, pp. 429-30.

[23] Pius XII, Allocution to the Sacred Roman Rota, Oct. 29, 1947—*AAS,* XXXIX (1947), 495-6; Bouscaren, *ibid.,* pp. 216, 218.

[24] Leo XIII, ep. encycl. *Immortale Dei—Fontes,* n. 592; *The Catholic Mind,* Nov. 8, 1936, p. 432.

D. *Objections*

In stating that its judicial power is "proper and exclusive," the Church places itself in square and inexorable opposition to the enemies of the Church who attack 1) its status in the sense of a juridically perfect society, and 2) the origin and 3) the nature of its jurisdiction.

1. The Church, therefore, condemns the doctrine of the would-be reformers and modernists who, in separating religion from the Church,

> [reject] entirely her title to the nature and rights of a perfect society . . . and . . . hold that she differs in no respect from other societies in the State, and for this reason possesses no right nor any legal power of action, save that which she holds by concession and favor of the government.[25]

To hold such a doctrine the modernists must reject the inspired testimony of the New Testament, and twenty centuries of Christian tradition and history, which clearly point out the fact of the foundation and existence of a visible, single, spiritual society, instituted by Christ for the salvation of all men.[26] Moreover, Cardinal Billot (1846-1931) pointed out that the reasoning which holds that a spiritual society is unnecessary, is philosophically false, because the higher the goal and the more removed it is from the senses the less well equipped is the individual, when left to himself to obtain that goal. A child, for example, needs more discipline and training to acquire learning and virtue, than to acquire skill in sports. But, since personal salvation, with its goal in an unseen and spiritual God, is a goal that is the highest and most removed from the human

---

[25] Leo XIII, ep. encycl. *Immortale Dei—Fontes,* n. 592, *The Catholic Mind,* Nov. 8, 1936, p. 438.

[26] This point forms the object of a particular branch of theology called apologetics, and is presupposed by the science of public ecclesiastical law. For further information any standard book of Catholic apologetics may be referred to such as: Billot, *Tractatus De Ecclesia Dei* (2 vols. in 1, 5. ed., Romae: Apud Aedes Universitatis Gregorianae, 1927); Yelle, *De Ecclesia et de Locis Theologicis* (Montreal: Grand Seminaire, 1945); Yelle et Fournier, *Apologetica* (Montreal: Grand Seminaire, 1945).

senses, it demands the aid and existence of a religious society which itself possesses a divine guidance and a divinely ratified authority.[27]

2. Equally to be condemned are those who, while admitting the utility of some sort of spiritual organization, reject the divine origin of the judicial power of the Church, and hold that this authority is derived either from the faithful or from the State.

Those who hold that the authority of the Church is derived from the faithful argue that this is so either, as Marsilius of Padua, Richer, and Febronius taught,[28] because Christ gave them this power, or, as Boehmer taught,[29] because of the contractual agreement, freely entered into as a natural right at the time of baptism, by which the faithful voluntarily ceded such rights to the society. There is, however no basis in fact for the theory that the faithful have such authority from Christ, for Christ clearly committed to a college of Apostles the rights and duties of preaching, of priestly ministry, and of social authority in order to enlighten, sanctify, and bring the faithful of the Church to the maturity of followers of Christ.[30] If the faithful have not received authority from Christ, neither do they have it of themselves. Since men who are bound to an end, are also bound

---

[27] Billot, *Tractatus de Ecclesia Christi,* I, 458-9.

[28] Cf. *supra,* pp. 73-75.

[29] Cf. *supra,* pp. 72-73.

[30] "Look at the words in which He communicated to them their powers: the power to offer sacrifice in remembrance of Him (Luke, 22:19), the power to forgive sins (John, 20:21-23), the promise and gift of the supreme power of the keys to Peter and to his Successors in person (Matthew, 16:10; John, 21:15-17), the communication to all the Apostles of the power to bind and to loose (Matthew, 18:18). Finally, ponder the words with which Christ, before His Ascension, transmitted to these same Apostles the universal commission which He received from the Father (Matthew, 28:18-20; John, 20:21). Is there anything in all this which can leave room for doubt or equivocation? The whole history of the Church, from its beginning to our own day, does not cease to echo those words and to give the same testimony with a clearness and precision which no subtlety can disturb or conceal. . . . There is not, therefore, and there cannot be in the Church, as it is founded by Christ, a popular tribunal or a judicial power deriving from the people." —Pius XII. Allocution to the Sacred Roman Rota, Oct. 2, 1945—*AAS,* XXXVII (1945), 259-61; Bouscaren, *The Canon Law Digest,* Supplement through 1948, pp. 211-13.

to all necessary and useful means to obtain that end, all men—for all men are bound to save their souls by divine law—are bound, at least *de iure,* by the Church, and consequently by its judicial power, as a necessary means and divine precept for salvation.[31] Therefore, the authority within this society does not derive through its members, either by divine delegation, or as a natural right, but from the divine law imposed upon all the members.

If the judicial power of the Church is not derived from the faithful, neither does it have its origins in the State, as Stephani and Grotius taught.[32] This is so, first, because the judicial power of the Church flows from the nature of the Church as a divinely constituted, juridically perfect society whose spiritual purposes and means are altogether distinct in character from those of the State; secondly, because the judicial activity of the Church was exercised even during the early persecutions when there could be no question of imperial concession; and, finally, because it is not merely the figment of medieval politics, based on a forged concession of the emperors, as some would wish, for the "Donation of Constantine" upon which this objection rests could furnish no foundation for the judicial power of the Church, both because the emperor as a temporal authority could not grant a spiritual power, for he possessed none, and because this false document, even before its authenticity was disproved, was never offered as more than a corroborative argument for the papal power, which rested solidly on theological and philosophical foundations.[33]

3. There are those who object that the very nature of the Church argues against its possession of a judicial power.

Among these are the Reformers who, in holding that religion is purely a spiritual, personal matter, interpret such texts as "Go, therefore, teaching them to observe all things whatsoever I have commanded you," [34] as vindicating merely a directive power, and not a true jurisdiction. The Church, so they contend, may teach, argue, criticize, advise, preach, but it remains without the possession of any enforceable judicial power.

---

[31] Cappello, *Summa Iuris Publici Ecclesiastici,* n. 103.

[32] Cf. *supra,* p. 72.

[33] Cf. *supra,* pp. 30-1; Cappello, *op. cit.,* nos. 132-144.

[34] Matthew 28:20.

Such arguments fail to take into consideration the context of this divine commission, for on that occasion Our Lord said, "All power is given to me in heaven and on earth. Go, therefore, . . . I am with you all days, even to the consummation of the world," as well as numerous other occasions on which real jurisdiction was bestowed upon the Apostles.[35] Moreover, pious exhortations are equally insufficient and ineffective in the maintenance of the social order and the welfare of the spiritual society, as they are in the civil society. This task requires the legitimate pronouncement and enforceable sentence of a real, authoritative, judicial power.[36]

Another argument against the judicial power of the Church is that its purpose, and therefore its power, must be purely spiritual in nature. The Church is concerned only with the interior dispositions of man, his conscience, his soul, his salvation. From this it is taken to follow that the Church has no social, judicial power outside of the internal forum of conscience, unless it receives it from the temporal authority of the State.

This line of reasoning is also false, because the nature of a society is not to be judged by its purpose alone, but by its purpose in conjunction with the means which it must use to obtain that purpose. In order to obtain its purpose, a society must have full control over all the necessary means. But the Church is not an association of spirits but of men. The worship of God, especially as a social obligation, and the salvation of souls necessitate the employment of ontologically material objects, such as churches and altars, schools and societies, which obtain a spiritual character through their ordination to a spiritual end. Therefore, the Church must have real social authority, exercised not only over the consciences of men, but over the external regulation and discipline of men and materials as well.[37] It follows, then, that there must exist two separate fora of jurisdiction in the Church, the one, that of conscience, and the other, that of an external, juridical relationship.[38]

---

35 Cf. *supra,* footnote 30, p. 94.

36 Cf. Suarez, *supra,* p. 69.

37 Tanquerey, *Synopsis Theologiae Dogmaticae Fundamentalis,* I, 648.

38 Cf. Pius XII, Allocution to the Sacred Roman Rota, Oct. 2, 1944—*AAS,* XXXVI (1944), 228; Bouscaren, *ibid.,* 239; also Cappello, *op. cit.,* nos. 134-5.

E. *Appeal from Alleged Abuses*

There are those, nevertheless, who, while not denying every shred of judicial authority to the Church, so misunderstand its proper and exclusive nature, as to maintain that recourse should be permitted from the ecclesiastical to the civil courts, especially in cases of abuse.[39]

While those who propose the doctrine of "appeal from alleged abuse" generally base themselves on a misunderstanding of the proper and exclusive nature of the judicial power of the Church as discussed immediately above, they find special arguments to support their position on the potential appeal to the secular courts.

The first, indeed, is a Pauline precedent, based upon the appeal of the Apostle to Caesar.[40] The sophism of this argument is obvious, however, for Paul appealed from one civil court to another, and not from the spiritual to the temporal power. Moreover, nothing can be deduced concerning the rights of the Church from his refusal to appear before the Jewish Court, for with the coming of the Redeemer that court had lost its legitimate spiritual authority.

Again, they appeal to tradition and antiquity, pointing to such cases as the appeal of the Arians and Donatists to the Emperor. Even here their reasoning is false, first, because they disregard the peculiar circumstances of the time,[41] and, secondly, because they offer the example of schismatics, from which no valid argument can be deduced as to the rights of the Church.

Appeal from supposed abuses is the product of regal absolutism,[42] but it is also inherent in the system of dis-establishment in what the State, failing to recognize the due authority established by God to maintain order in the spiritual society, becomes the sole and ultimate authority for maintaining all peace and social order, and must, therefore, assume an indirect power, or police power, over even spiritual affairs.[43]

---

39 Cf. the Statutes of Clarendon, *supra.* p. 64; the post-Reformation Regalism of Richer, Febronius, etc., *supra,* pp. 74-5; the doctrine of the American courts, *supra,* pp. 83-4.

40 Cf. *supra,* p. 25.

41 Cf. *supra,* pp. 27-30.

42 Cf. *supra,* pp. 74-5.

43 Cf. *Supra,* pp. 81-84.

This function of the State is not altogether disadvantageous to the Church since it provides a means by which the Church may obtain due assistance from the State against contumacious and rebellious subjects, as in such matters as controversies over the possession of schismatic churches. Furthermore, since the Church maintains a complete system of appeal courts, and sound judicial principles and laws, it has little to fear in the way of appeals because of abusive treatment from those who stand before her tribunals.

Fundamentally, of course, the system of "appeal from abuse" cannot be considered as other than an infraction of the rights of the Church, for it is a violation of the fundamental principles as established by Christ. Appeal implies recourse from an inferior to a superior judge of the same competence and order. Appeal from an ecclesiastical judge to a civil judge complies with neither of these requirements.

The jurisdiction of each court is bounded by the juridical status and order of the society from which it receives its authorization. The law must be applied by the same authority which promulgates it.[44] The civil courts, for instance, have no right either to apply military law, or to judge military matters or personnel. The civil courts are completely distinct from the military courts. Lacking jurisdiction in cases of the first instance, they have no appellate jurisdiction, nor any right of surveillance of, or interference with, the military court.[45] Similarly, the civil and ecclesiastical courts are as distinct as the societies themselves, each receiving independent jurisdiction from the divine law, either natural or positive, the one for matters spiritual, the other for matters temporal. The civil court, then, lacks not only

---

[44] Ottaviani, *Compendium,* n. 249.

[45] Coronata, *Ius Publicum Ecclesiasticum,* n. 141. This analogy is not quite perfect in American law, for military law is a "part of municipal law . . . superadded to the ordinary law . . . [and] regulates the military conduct of men in the land and naval forces at all times and all places, in time of peace and during war."—Smith, *Handbook of Elementary Law,* pp. 129, 381; but cf. also p. 366, where in explaining the elements of jurisdiction it is stated, "A judgment made by a court without jurisdiction is void. To render its judgment valid and its jurisdiction complete . . . the court must have jurisdiction over the subject of the action and the res or property in contest." Hence the principle remains valid.

the right to review the acts and decisions of an ecclesiastical tribunal on the merits of the case (simple appeal), but the right of any interference with, or surveillance of, the manner in which this tribunal has acted, even though it appears to have acted negligently or unjustly (appeal from abuse). Such an act on the part of the civil authorities would be invalid and irregular, for it would be an exceeding of due authority, and a destroying of the distinctness which exists between these separate juridical orders by the will of Christ Himself.

To argue that the faithful may not receive adequate justice at the hands of the ecclesiastical court is to insult and outrage the character of those whose lives are a dedicated labor of love for the truth and justice of Christ. It is to ignore the whole organic system of appeal constituted within the framework of the government of the Church, by which the Church protects its members from any possible negligence or biased abuse at the hands of an individual judge or tribunal. It is to throttle religious freedom, and to subject it to the very real possibility of a political tyranny and prejudiced fanaticism.

Further, judicial appeal implies recourse from a lower to a higher authority. But the ecclesiastical judge has proper and exclusive authority in all matters pertaining to the spiritual, while the Church is indirectly superior to the State in temporalities by virtue of the greater nobility of its purpose, and the sacredness of its origin.[46] Appeal to the State, then, is juridically unprincipled, because it perverts the right order by allowing a lower authority to override the decisions of a higher one. "Or does it seem just to you that the spirit should yield to the flesh, that the celestial should be governed by the terrestrial, that the human should be preferred to the divine?" [47]

But in exercising the "appeal from abuse," the State may claim that it seeks only to protect the material and civil rights of its citizens, such as their material goods and money in religious ventures, or their honor and reputation.

Those who hold this duty to be incumbent upon the State fail to recognize that the citizen is also a child of God, that the duty of the State is to protect the citizen in so far as he is a citizen subject to the

[46] Cf. Bellarmine and Suarez, *supra,* pp. 66-70.

[47] St. Gregory Nazianzenus—c. 6, D. X; cf. *supra,* p. 41, footnote n. 8.

State, but in so far as he is a child of God, a member of the Church, he is beyond the due limits of temporal jurisdiction. In spiritual matters he is subject to the authority of God and His Church alone.[48]

Furthermore it is to be denied that these temporal interests are exclusively temporal. The temporal or spiritual character of objects are not to be determined by their ontological nature, or physical make-up, but rather by the use or purpose for which they are employed. If temporal and natural objects are used for spiritual and ecclesiastical purposes, they become subject to the jurisdiction of the Church, just as non-corporeal things are subject to the State when used for its purposes. Therefore, the penalties inflicted upon a member of the Church for his spiritual welfare, or for the common good of the spiritual society, though they be material or temporal in nature, are legitimate objects of ecclesiastical authority.[49]

A further argument for non-interference on the part of the civil authority has been adduced by civil judges themselves.

> Church tribunals are better judges of the ecclesiastical law than civil courts can ever be. After pointing out that the various associated church organizations each have a body of constitutional and ecclesiastical law to be found in their constitutions, books of discipline, collections of precedents and usages and customs that task 'the ablest minds to become familiar with,' the court concludes that to allow an appeal from the decisions of their church tribunals to the civil courts would permit 'an appeal from the more learned tribunal in the law which should decide the case, to one which is less so.' [50]

The Church, then, has condemned "appeal from alleged abuse" as an insidious error and an intolerable injustice. As far back as the Council of Antioch (341), the Church threatened to excommunicate those who dared to appeal, in contravention of the precepts of the sacred canons, from the ecclesiastical judge to the civil authority.[51] In his Bull *Unam Sanctam*,[52] Boniface VIII (1294-1303) echoed the

---

[48] Ottaviani, *Institutiones Iuris Publici Ecclesiastici*, II, 267-9, footnote 10.

[49] Cf. Coronata, *Ius Publicum Ecclesiasticum*, nos. 182-3.

[50] Zollmann, *American Civil Church Law*, p. 207, referring to the case: *Fort v. First Baptist Church of Paris*, 55 S W, 402, 406 (Tex.).

[51] Cans. 11, 12 (Mansi, II, col. 1314).

[52] Cf. *supra*, pp. 60-2.

sentiment of Constantine the Great on the matter of civil judgments over spiritual matters and men,[53] when he stated: "If there is a deviation of the terrestrial power, it will be judged by the spiritual power; but if there is a deviation on the part of a lower spiritual agency, it shall be judged by the higher one; but if there deviate the supreme spiritual power, it can be judged, not by man, but by God alone."[54] The error was likewise condemned both in the Council of Trent (1545-1563),[55] and in the *Syllabus* of Pius IX (1864).[56]

The present law censures the appeal of a case of the mixed forum to the secular court after it has been brought before an ecclesiastical judge, with the penalties thought necessary by the ordinary in the manner specified in canon 2222, and with forfeiture of the right to bring action in the ecclesiastical forum against the same person in the same case or in any matter connected with the case.[57] It also imposes *ipso facto* an excommunication, reserved in a special way to the Holy See, upon those who either directly or indirectly impede the exercise of ecclesiastical jurisdiction in the internal or external forum by having recourse for that purpose to any secular authority,[58] as well as upon those who have recourse to the secular power for the purpose of impeding any letter or acts issued by the Apostolic See or its legates, or of directly or indirectly preventing their publication or execution.[59]

---

53 Cf. p. 27.

54 Denzinger, n. 469; Ottaviani, *Institutiones Iuris Publici Ecclesiastici,* II, 267.

55 Conc. Trident., sess. XXV, *de ref.,* c. 3. Schroeder, *Canons and Decrees of the Council of Trent* (St. Louis: B. Herder Co., 1941).

56 Prop. 41—Denzinger, n. 1741.

57 Can. 1554.

58 Can. 2334, 2°.

59 Can. 2333. Moreover, clerics who violate canon 2334 are punished with the additional penalties of suspension from, or even deprivation of, any benefice, office, dignity, pension, or position which he may hold in the Church. Religious are deprived of office and of the right to cast or receive a vote in a canonical election, and may be punished with other penalties in accordance with their constitutions.—Can. 2336, § 1.

CHAPTER VI

THE PROPER AND EXCLUSIVE JURISDICTION OF THE CHURCH IN CONTENTIOUS MATTERS

The jurisdictional rights of a juridically perfect society are established on a threefold basis: the nature of the case, the status of the parties, and territorial location.[1] Of these three the last is irrelevant, since the jurisdiction of the Church is territorially universal.[2] The legislation of the Church first determines the grounds of jurisdiction which belong to its exclusive and proper province by reason of the nature of the case, treating of contentious and criminal matters in that order, and then proceeds to determine its competence according to the juridic status of the persons.

The principle applicable in the establishing of the juridic character of an object, and hence of the objects and limits of the judicial power of the Church, is the principle of finality: *talis finis qualis auctoritas*. A perfect society has a native, or proper, and so an inalienable right to regulate, judge, and administer all the means necessary and useful for its purposes. The proper jurisdiction of a perfect society over any given matter is, therefore, established by the relationship of the matter as a means, or an impediment, to the proper ends of the society. This jurisdiction is also exclusive if the relationship of the means to the end is such that the finality of the matter, or its effects, are referred directly to one order, or one society, alone.[3]

The Church, then, by reason of its status as a divinely instituted, juridically perfect society, which has been given sole charge over the sanctification and salvation of men as its proper and exclusive object, claims proper and exclusive jurisdiction over all contentious cases which are directly and exclusively referred as means or impediments

[1] Cf. Roberti, *Iuris Processualis Compendium*, n. 191.

[2] Matthew, 28:18-20.

[3] Cf. *supra*, pp. 15-16.

to the accomplishment of its purpose. These matters are spiritual or annexed to the spiritual.

A. *Spiritual Matters*

> The Almighty has appointed the charge of the human race between two powers, the ecclesiastical and the civil, the one being set over divine, and the other over human things. Each in its kind is supreme, each has fixed limits within which it is contained, limits which are defined by the nature and special object of the province of each, so that there is, we may say, an orbit traced out within which the action of each is brought into play by its own native right. . . . Whatever, therefore, in things human is of sacred character, whatever belongs either of its own nature or by reason of the end to which it is referred, to the salvation of souls, or to the worship of God, is subject to the power and judgment of the Church. Whatever is to be ranged under the civil and political order is rightly subject to the civil authority. Jesus Christ has himself given the command that what is Caesar's is to be rendered to Caesar, and that what belongs to God is to be rendered to God.[4]

The spiritual character of a matter is constituted by its spiritual finality, by its relationship as a means helpful or detrimental to the ends proper to the spiritual society. It does not matter whether the objects are ontologically material or spiritual;[5] nor whether they are supernatural by nature, v.g., the sacraments, or by elevation through divine positive legislation, v.g., sacramental marriage, or through human ecclesiastical legislation, as by consecration;[6] nor whether they serve immediately in the worship of God and the conferral of grace, for the physical life and sustenance of the Church, or both, and are accordingly classified by canon 726 as spiritual, temporal, and mixed.[7] Hence all matters which are helpful or harm-

[4] Leo XIII, ep. encycl. *Immortale Dei—Fontes,* n. 592, *The Catholic Mind,* Nov. 8, 1936, pp. 431-2.

[5] Cf. *supra,* p. 100.

[6] Ottaviani, *Compendium,* n. 226; also, Suarez, *supra,* p. 16, footnote 51.

[7] Care must be taken not to confuse this division of matters into spiritual, temporal, and mixed, as used in canon 726, with the same terminology as used in public ecclesiastical law. Public law is concerned with the division of matters according to their relationship of finality between the Church and the State. Canon 726 is concerned with the finality of means within

ful to the worship of God, the salvation of souls, and the welfare of the Church, pertain to the proper end, and consequently the proper jurisdiction, of the Church.

Furthermore, since judicial competence is not only established by, but also limited according to, the principle of finality, those objects which are dedicated solely to the service of God and the Church, by being withdrawn entirely from all temporal utility and finality, fall not only under the proper, but also the exclusive, jurisdiction of the Church. In such cases there is created an absolute incompetency, rendering any judicial activity of the State upon these matters null and void. It has no basis for authority in these matters through either the finality of the object, or the efficient causality of the power of the Church.[8] Indeed, the nobler and more essential finality of the Church, which places the Church on a higher level than the State, eliminates the possibility of even an indirect intervention of the State in such matters.[9] The State, then, is absolutely incompetent to judge any purely spiritual matter, even when contained as an incidental issue, in its courts.

A question arises regarding the rights of the State in judging the prejudicial questions of a spiritual nature connected with temporal cases brought before the civil tribunal. Obviously the State has no right to judge a spiritual controversy, as, for instance, the validity of a Catholic marriage or baptism. It is therefore the duty of the State to refer such questions to the proper ecclesiastical tribunal, and to base its decisions concerning the temporal matter on the finding of this tribunal.[10]

If, however, the question involves no dispute concerning the religious question, but simply a question of bare fact—did this person undergo a ceremony of baptism?—the State may decide the point, for

---

the Church alone. The Church will have proper and exclusive jurisdiction over even temporal matters in the sense of this canon, provided that they have no effect on civil society, while it may not have such jurisdiction even over spiritual matters in the sense of this canon, if there are separable temporal effects flowing from it. Cf. Coronata, *Institutiones Iuris Canonici,* II, nos. 706-7.

8 Cf. *supra,* pp. 88-92.

9 Cf. *supra,* footnote 33, p. 68; 98-100.

10 Lega-Bartoccetti, *Commentarius in Iudicia Ecclesiastica,* I, 78.

in doing so it is not judging a spiritual matter as spiritual, but merely as a material, sensible point of fact. In most cases, indeed, the civil court will be but accepting the testimony of church records or judicial sentences of the ecclesiastical officials as qualified and competent authorities.[11]

A question of this type which arose quite frequently in history, and which was the source of much abuse and bitter quarrels, concerned the right of the State to judge the facts of canonical possession of a benefice or of patronal rights, which items arose as questions prejudicial to the temporal rights involved. Ecclesiastical authors agree, however, that in such a situation, the State is not competent to judge even the bare fact of possession, because it is inextricable from the spiritual. The temporal rights are here not separable, but inseparable, from the spiritual substance, for they are an integral part of a benefice.[12] In the event that a civil court should judge against the fact of canonical possession on the part of a certain cleric, it would inevitably disturb the whole spiritual order by casting doubts upon the validity of all spiritual, jurisdictional rights and acts of the incumbent, for the cleric could not possess the spiritual rights apart from the temporal rights annexed thereto. Therefore the State is incompetent to judge even the bare fact of canonical possession of benefices, patronal rights, and other spiritual rights to which temporal rights are inextricably annexed.[13]

---

[11] Cf. Lega-Bartoccetti, *ibid.*, I, 14, 77; art. 3, 15; Cavagnis, *Institutiones Iuris Publici Ecclesiastici,* I, nos. 436-41; Cappello, *Summa Iuris Publici Ecclesiastici,* nos. 255-7.

[12] "An ecclesiastical benefice is a jurdicial entity, permanently constituted or erected by the competent ecclesiastical authority, and consisting of a sacred office and the right to receive the revenue accruing from the endowment of such office."—Can. 1409.

[13] Cavagnis, *op. cit.,* nos. 438-41; Cappello, *op. cit.,* n. 256; Marchesi, *Summula Iuris Publici Ecclesiastici,* n. 66; Coronata, *Ius Publicum Ecclesiasticum,* n. 88. Bouix held with Schmalzgrueber, however, that if the patronal rights were but one item in a judgment against a property owner, as in cases of bankruptcy, the State had the indirect power to judge regarding the possession of the patronal rights. Cf. Bouix, *Tractatus de Iudiciis Ecclesiasticis,* I, 115-6.

B. *Matters Annexed to the Spiritual*

> The Almighty has appointed the charge of the human race between two powers, the ecclesiastical and the civil, the one being set over divine, and the other over human things. . . . But in as much as each of these two powers has authority over the same subjects, and as it might come to pass that one and the same thing—related differently, but still remaining one and the same thing—might belong to the jurisdiction and determination of both, therefore God, who foresees all things, and who is the Author of these two powers, has marked out the course of each in right correlation to the other. . . . The nature and scope of that connection can be determined only, as We have laid down, by having regard to the nature of each power, and by taking account of the relative excellence and nobleness of their purpose and occasions when rulers of the State and the Roman Pontiff come to an understanding touching some special matter.[14]

1. Notion of *Res Mixta*

Not all means used by the Church for its divine mission are so completely withdrawn and dedicated to the service of God and the Church as to lose entirely every temporal aspect and finality. It is as impossible to isolate completely the spiritual from the temporal as to separate body from soul. The spiritual destiny of man depends upon the manner in which he conducts his earthly life. The Church, as a society of men, has need not only of those sacred things which are employed immediately in the worship of God and the conferral of grace, but even of such material items as real estate and trust funds for the sustenance and maintenance of the physical life of the Church as a society of and for men.

It is little wonder, then, that innumerable objects serve neither a purely spiritual, nor yet a purely temporal, purpose. They contain both juridic elements. They are a mixture of the two, and consequently are subject to the legitimate interest and jurisdiction of both the Church and the State.

Some of these affect both societies directly and under the same aspect, as cases which, while properly temporal, have been conceded to the jurisdiction of the Church by concordat; others affect both

[14] Leo XIII, ep. encycl. *Immortale Dei—Fontes*, n. 592; *The Catholic Mind*, Nov. 8, 1936, pp. 431-2.

societies directly, but under divergent aspects, as matrimony in its various derivable effects.

The first classification does not pertain to both societies because of any intrinsic mixture of character. The mixture comes from the exterior, from the over-lapping, common interests and finality of the societies themselves. This over-lapping finality may be natural and proper, as, for example, the cumulative rights over a temporal matter contained as an incidental issue in a spiritual case; or accidental, i.e., not by native right, but by contingence simply upon the will and the concession of the social authorities, as in matters of concordats.[15] The jurisdictional rights over such matters then may be proper, but never exclusive by their nature, inasmuch as either of the societies obtains exclusive jurisdiction only in individual cases through the principle of "first arrival."[16] Such matters, then, being mixed by reason of the over-lapping finality of both societies rather than by any intrinsic mixture of their character, are called *res mixti fori,* matters of the mixed forum.

The second classification of objects, i.e., those which affect both societies directly, but under divergent aspects, have an intrinsically mixed character. They possess a double finality, two distinct effects, one spiritual, the other temporal. They obtain this double finality either because their substance, i.e., their constitutive element or essence, directly and immediately pertains to both orders, or because of some connected effect pertaining to the alternate society. They form, then, a distinct classification from the *res mixti fori* and are called *res mixtae,* matters of mixed character. They are defined as those matters which are directly referred to a twofold end, spiritual and temporal, and according to either respect are under the disposition of the competent society.[17]

---

[15] The purely arbitrary concessions and delegation of jurisdiction which may be treated in concordats is beyond the aim, or even the possibility, of treatment in this thesis. The principles of jurisdiction discussed here are based strictly upon the character and finality of the objects and societies in question.

[16] "In causis in quibus tum Ecclesia tum civilis potestas aeque competentes sunt, quaeque dicuntur mixti fori, est locus praeventionis."—Can. 1553, § 2.

[17] Ottaviani, *Compendium,* n. 224; Cappello, *Summa Iuris Publici Ecclesiastici,* n. 251; Goldsmith, *The Competence of Church and State over Marriage—Disputed Points,* p. 21.

2. Types of *Res Mixtae*

Since the governing principle of juridical competence is still that of finality, and since the *res mixtae* substantially relate to one society, obtaining their double finality through annexed effects, it is necessary to consider the nature of both substance and effects, and to distinguish carefully between the effects themselves in the determination of jurisdictional rights. For this purpose *res mixtae* are divided first by reason of the finality of their substances into natural and supernatural (or supernaturalized),[18] and then by reason of their effects into inseparable and separable.[19]

3. Jurisdictional Principles Governing the *Res Mixtae*

a) Since *res mixtae* are referred directly to the spiritual and the temporal orders under divergent aspects, the jurisdictional rights over such matters are not cumulative and over-lapping, as in the case of the *res mixti fori,* but proper and exclusive, in accordance with the general principle of finality which governs and distinguishes all jurisdictional relationships between Church and State.[20]

b) The jurisdictional right in question will always concern an effect which is referred to the society alternate to that to which the substance pertains. If this were not so, there would be no question of a *res mixta.*

It cannot be concluded immediately, however, that such an effect will necessarily pertain to the jurisdiction of that alternate society. It must be remembered that the effect is always annexed to, and consequent upon, the substance, whose finality has already given one society an established interest and right in the matter. The finality of an effect is itself, therefore, always twofold. It has a relationship not only to the alternate society, but also to the society having

---

18 Cf. *supra,* pp. 15-16; 104-5.

19 Concerning the division of *res mixtae,* and also the question of the *res mixti fori,* cf. Coronata, *Ius Publicum Ecclesiasticum,* nos. 83, 87; Ottaviani, *Compendium,* nos. 225-6; Cappello, *Summa Iuris Publici Ecclesiastici,* n. 251; Lega-Bartoccetti, *Commentarius in Iudicia Ecclesiastica,* I, 11-14; Goldsmith, *The Competence of Church and State over Marriage—Disputed Points,* pp. 21-2.

20 Can. 1553, §§ 1-2; Ottaviani, *Compendium,* n. 224.

jurisdiction over the substance from which it is derived. It is this latter relationship, as the more immediate and more essential, though perhaps the less apparent, which exists as the primary factor for any determining of the finality of an effect. Hence it is the relationship of effect to substance which takes precedence in limiting and governing the jurisdictional rights over a *res mixta* when the alternate society is absolutely incompetent in relation to the substance, as it does in the case of temporal effects flowing from a Christian marriage.

c) Natural *res mixtae,* such as the education of youth are referred directly by the nature of their substance, or by annexed spiritual effects, to both the spiritual and the temporal orders, so that each society has a proper and exclusive jurisdiction according to the proper and distinct finality contained therein. Jurisdiction over the spiritual effects is in no way affected by their annexation as an incidental, or even as a prejudicial, issue to a temporal substance, for the State is absolutely incompetent to judge spiritual matters either directly or indirectly, as principal cases, or as incidental issues.[21]

d) In their relationship to a spiritual substance, temporal effects may be annexed inseparably, i.e., they may flow from its very essence or nature as natural and necessary properties, conditions, or effects. In such cases the spiritual question is always prejudicial to the temporal point at issue, which cannot be decided apart from contact with the substance itself. Controversies concerning the income from benefices, the legitimacy of offspring, the freedom for remarriage, and the like, all hinge necessarily upon the spiritual substance itself. In doing so they take on the juridic character of the substance itself according to the principle: *accessorium sequitur principale,* so as to become juridically composite and inseparable elements of the whole. It immediately becomes apparent, then, that if the substance of a *res mixta* is supernatural, or supernaturalized, all the necessary, or inseparable effects annexed thereto belong to the same proper and exclusive jurisdiction as the spiritual substance itself. These, then,

---

[21] Coronata, *Ius Publicum Ecclesiasticum,* n. 87; Cappello, *Summa Iuris Publici Ecclesiastici,* n. 253, III; Cavagnis, *Institutiones Iuris Publici Ecclesiastici,* I, n. 426; Ottaviani, *Compendium,* n. 228.

are the matters annexed to the spiritual over which the Church claims a proper and exclusive jurisdiction in canon 1553.[22]

e) On the other hand, those effects which, as separable from the spiritual substance, do not flow necessarily from its essence or nature, though perhaps it may be quite natural for them to do so, and which depend mainly upon human acts and positive legislation for their existence, can be juridically disjoined from the substance, and so fall under the competence of the alternate society. Inheritance rights, for example, are natural but not necessary effects of marriage. Questions concerning the validity of a will, or regarding the proportional division of property in cases in which a person dies intestate, are purely temporal in character, and subject to the positive legislation and judgment of the civil authority. They may therefore be juridically separated from the spiritual substance inherent in matrimony as a sacrament, and their temporal finality will not be restricted in consequence of their relationship with the sacrament of matrimony. If, however, the right of inheritance raises the prejudicial question of legitimacy, which itself is spiritual in nature through its inseparable annexation to the spiritual question of the legitimacy of the marriage, the right of inheritance will in turn become spiritual by reason of an inseparable annexation, in the sense that judgment must be reserved until the question of legitimacy has been settled by the Church.

The jurisdiction of the Church over such temporal, separable matters, when they arise as incidental questions contained in spiritual cases before its courts, belongs to its proper, though not exclusive, jurisdiction.[23] It is precisely in these matters, which are of no direct interest to the Church, and which see no change in their temporal nature through the fact that they arise in conjunction with a spiritual case, that the classification of objects called *res mixti fori* arises.

The claim of the Church to the proper right of indirectly judging

[22] Ottaviani, *Compendium*, n. 90; Marchesi, *Summula Iuris Publici Ecclesiastici*, n. 65, I; Cappello, *Summa Iuris Publici Ecclesiastici*, nos. 252-3; Coronata, *Ius Publicum Ecclesiasticum*, n. 87; Cavagnis, *Institutiones Iuris Publici Ecclesiastici*, I, n. 429.

[23] "Causae de effectibus matrimonii mere civilibus, si principaliter agantur, pertinent ad civilem magistratum ad normam can. 1016; sed si incidenter et accessorie, possunt etiam a iudice ecclesiastico ex propria potestate cognosci ac definiri."—Can. 1961.

these cases, i.e., of judging them as incidental cases, rest 1) on the existence of an indirect relationship to such matters created by their relationship to a spiritual substance; 2) on the indirect aid to the spiritual welfare of the parties, which comes from the regulation of temporal problems annexed to their spiritual controversies; 3) on the fact that there is no essential disruption of the juridical order, since the Church is indirectly superior to the State; 4) on the fact that the juridical order may be benefitted and preserved through a prevention of confusion and contradictions between civil and ecclesiastical decisions, and through a saving for both the civil authorities and the parties of the time, labor, and expense of instituting a second trial in the civil courts; 5) on the normality of a judge's completing the case which he has begun, and indeed in all of its ramifications; and, finally, 6) on the age-long tradition which began with the approbation of St. Paul: "Do you not know that we shall judge angels? How much more worldly things!" (I Corinthians, 6:3-4).[24]

But while such activity is proper to the Church, the Church, even in the ages of established Christendom, undertook the settlement of such questions reluctantly, because such matters pertained more directly to the civil authority, and the Church did not wish to appear as usurping the authority of the State.[25]

The Church is careful to respect the proper and exclusive right of the civil power to judge all matters that are strictly temporal in character. Even in those which are separably annexed to spiritual matters the Church is careful not to intervene directly. If such questions arise as the principal point at issue, the Church regards them as pertaining to the civil magistrate,[26] with the principle of "first arrival" applying only if both the civil and the ecclesiastical judges are "equally competent," which of course they are not in the direct adjudication of temporal matters.[27]

---

[24] Cf. Cappello, *Summa Iuris Publici Ecclesiastici*, nos. 220-6, 258; Billot, *Tractatus de Ecclesia Christi*, II, 76-81; Lega-Bartoccetti, *Commentarius in Iudicia Ecclesiastica*, I, 14, 75, 79; art. 19, 1; Bouix, *Tractatus de Iuridiciis Ecclesiasticis*, I, 116.

[25] Cf. *supra*, pp. 52-3; Lega-Bartoccetti, *Commentarius in Iudicia Ecclesiastica*, I, 15-16; can. 1961.

[26] Can. 1961.

[27] Can. 1553, § 2.

Any attempt of the ecclesiastical judges to concern themselves with purely temporal matters in our day, when jurisdictional rights are decided strictly according to the principle of finality, would be null and void, unless such jurisdiction devolves upon the Church in consequence of the simultaneous existence of three practically impossible conditions as deduced from history and tradition by ecclesiastical jurists.[28] These conditions are: 1) complete failure of the civil authority; 2) the impossibility of restoring a due civil process, and 3) the existence of an indirect spiritual finality.

1. If the civil authority operates normally, there is no basis for any interference by the Church in temporalities, for the Church must respect what is Caesar's. There are rare times, however, when the judicial power of the civil authority cannot, or will not, function. Such a situation could be occasioned by an inter-regnum, when, because of political instability, turmoil, or revolution, no legitimate or effective civil authority exists; by negligence, subornation, or prejudice of the civil judges; by their inability to reach a definitive sentence; by the existence of a case of equity when there is no legal protection afforded by the civil law; or by the poverty, weakness, or helplessness of victims who cannot obtain justice civilly.[29]

2. The first condition is not sufficiently fulfilled if the civil process can be produced in any way. The interest and jurisdiction of the Church in temporal matters are but secondary and indirect. Hence the primary duty incumbent upon the Church when faced with the absence, impotency, or neglect of the civil authority, is not that of assuming temporal authority immediately, but rather one of assistance in restoring effective force and respect for the normal, legitimate agency; to stir the negligent or corrupt judge to render equitable justice; to appeal, if possible, to a higher civil authority than that which has failed. It is only when all means for the normal settlement of these cases have been exhausted that the Church becomes invested with the duty and right to judge temporalities.

---

[28] Lega-Bartoccetti, *Commentarius in Iudicia Ecclesiastica,* I, 15-16; Bouix, *Tractatus de Iudiciis Ecclesiasticis,* I, 90-3; Cappelo, *Summa Iuris Publici Ecclesiastici,* n. 230; Marchesi, *Summula Iuris Publici Ecclesiastici,* pp. 76-7.

[29] Cf. *supra,* pp. 46-7; Bouix, *op. cit.,* I, 90-1.

Even in these cases the Church is not over-anxious to intervene in temporal matters, and so as a general rule, it will undertake such action only at the insistent request of an injured party.[30]

3. The rights of the Church are ever bounded by the principle of finality, and therefore before the ecclesiastical judge acquires a devolved temporal jurisdiction, even under such circumstances, at least an indirect spiritual finality must be established. In the unlikely hypothesis of the absolute failure of all legitimate temporal power, this latter condition is almost automatically fulfilled, for it pertains to the spiritual welfare of the faithful, and of the Church itself, that justice be rendered, and peace and order be maintained, even in purely temporal disputes and crimes. Especially during turbulent political periods do lawlessness and moral laxity abound, affecting not only the spiritual life of the delinquent, but infecting other members of the community as well, so that these matters easily pertain to the social welfare and authority of the Church.

Therefore in the total absence or negligence of all due temporal power, the duty and right to supply for this lamentable defect devolves upon the Church as the only extant divinely constituted authority.[31] In the words of Bellarmine, "The pope, as pope, cannot ordinarily judge temporal affairs, for Bernard rightly says, 'Here below and on earth these have their own judges, the kings and princes of the land. Why invade the territory of others? Why extend your scythe into another's harvest?' . . . But, nonetheless, in a case in which it is necessary for the salvation of souls, the pontiff can preside even over temporal judicial trials." [32]

C. *Summary of Principles Governing the Object and Limits of the Judicial Power of the Church in Contentious Matters*

1. The Church has proper and exclusive jurisdiction over all matters which are purely spiritual by reason of their finality. The State has proper jurisdiction over all matters which in similar fashion are

---

[30] Cf. Bouix, *op. cit.*, I, 92-3.

[31] Bouix, *op. cit.*, I, 91; Cappello, *Summa Iuris Publici Ecclesiastici*, n. 227; Lega-Bartoccetti, *op. cit.*, I, 13.

[32] *De Romano Pontifice*, Lib. V, Cap. VI (*Opera Omnia*, I, 532).

purely temporal. This jurisdiction is also exclusive, except in the rare event of a complete failure of all due civil authority, when because of spiritual consequences such jurisdiction devolves upon the Church.

2. In matters of mixed character each society has proper and exclusive judicial rights over the divergent aspects, according to their spiritual or temporal finality. This finality is affected by the relationship of effect to substance in spiritual matters.

3. In natural matters of mixed character, the State has jurisdiction over the substance, and over the annexed temporal effects. The Church has proper and exclusive jurisdiction over the annexed spiritual effects.

4. In spiritual, or spiritualized, matters of mixed character, the Church has proper and exclusive jurisdiction over the substance, over the annexed spiritual effects, and over the annexed, inseparable, temporal effects. Church and State have a proper, cumulative jurisdiction over the annexed, temporal, separable effects.

CHAPTER VII

THE PROPER AND EXCLUSIVE JUDICIAL POWER OF THE CHURCH IN CRIMINAL MATTERS

The Church has a proper and exclusive judicial power over the violations of ecclesiastical laws, and over all other acts in which sin is involved, in so far as the decision of guilt and the infliction of ecclesiastical penalties are concerned.[1]

A. *Function of the Judicial Power in regard to Criminal Matters*

Judicial power is concerned with the achieving of order in society, not only in regard to the rights of the members of the society, which it accomplishes through the settlement of controversies and disputes concerning the application of laws and facts (contentious trials), but also in regard to the public order of the community through the prosecution and punishment of those who violate its laws (criminal trials).[2]

These violations of the law with which the criminal trials are concerned are called delicts or crimes.[3] They can be distinguished, as they are in the civil courts, into delicts in the strict or broad sense of the term, accordingly as they are public or private wrongs. Delicts in the strict term, called crimes in civil law, give rise to actions instituted by the public authority for the purpose of punishing the wrongdoer in the public interest. Delicts in the broad sense, called torts in civil law, giving rise to contentious actions instituted by the individual victims in order to render wrongdoers liable to restitution for damages.[4] However, since both are violations of the law, and

---

[1] Can. 1553, § 1, 2°.

[2] Cans. 1552, § 2; 2210.

[3] In canon law, delicts and crimes are synonymous. In civil law crimes are distinguished into felonies and misdemeanors according to the seriousness of the offense and the consequent penalties attached. Cf. Coronata, *Institutiones Juris Canonici,* V. n. 1639; Smith, *Handbook of Elementary Law,* p. 156.

[4] Cf. Coronata, *op. cit.,* V, n. 1641; Smith, *op. cit.,* p. 149.

since violations of, or damage to, private rights redound upon the social order itself, the jurisdictional rights over delicts, whether in the strict or in the broad sense, are governed by the same principles.

Ultimately it is only the decision of the legislator that determines whether an act is or is not harmful to the social order itself, and this decision is embodied in the attachment of penalties to a law by the legislator.[5] It is for this reason that the Code defines delicts by their results, or penal consequences, as external and morally culpable violations of those laws to which at least an indeterminate penalty is attached.[6]

While the civil law adheres strictly to the principle: *nullum crimen sine lege; nulla poena sine lege,* the Church gives a somewhat broader interpretation to the concept of delicts and penal law. Unlike the departmental forms of government common to modern civil societies, those who possess jurisdiction in the Church simultaneously possess a legislative, a judicial, and an executive power.[7] Therefore, in addition to the general penal laws of the Church as established in the Code, it is left to the prudent discretion of the legitimate religious superiors to punish transgressions which carry no canonical penalty, but which they consider to be gravely harmful to the social order, by attaching proportionate penalties,[8] either by particular law, or by precept,[9] or even apart from any previous warning if the emerging scandal or resulting gravity of a particular crime call for such measures.[10]

B. *Jurisdictional Principles*

Inasmuch as it is the function of the judiciary, in criminal matters, to restore public order by declaring and imposing medicinal and punitive penalties, the principles of canon 1553 in regard to criminal affairs are inextricably bound to, and supplemented by, the correla-

---

[5] Cf. Regatillo, *Institutiones Iuris Canonici* (2 vols. Santander, 1949), II, n. 869.

[6] Can. 2195, § 1.

[7] Cf. cans. 196; 218; 1569; 329; 1572.

[8] Can. 2221.

[9] Can. 2220, § 1.

[10] Can. 2222, § 1.

tive canon on the coactive, or punitive, power of the Church. This canon, 2198, states:

> An offense which violates solely the law of the Church is by its nature subject to punishment by the ecclesiastical authority alone, although this authority may at times ask the assistance of the civil power, when it judges such aid necessary or opportune.
>
> An offense which violates solely a law of the civil society is by nature subject to punishment by that authority according to its own law, except that, in accordance with canon 120, clerics are to be tried in the ecclesiastical courts only, and the Church also is competent to judge it by reason of the sin committed.
>
> An offense which violates the law of both the Church and the State may be punished by either of the two powers.

From this canon it appears that the relative competence of Church and State over delicts, not only in coactive power, but in the judicial power by which penalties are imposed, is determined by the principle of finality, just as in contentious matters. Again the objects of the judicial power are divisible into spiritual, temporal, and mixed, according to their harmful effects upon the social order of one, or the other, or both, societies, as determined by the nature of the offense, and by their respective penal laws. Again the judicial power of Church and State, as of juridically perfect societies, extends properly and exclusively over the delicts which are their sole respective concerns. Again, there are crimes which affect both societies, either under divergent aspects, such as the violation of sepulchres (mixed delicits), or as harmful to both orders and both societies indiscriminately, as violations of the natural, moral law, when determined and penalized by the positive laws of the two societies (delicits of the mixed forum).

As in contentious matters, so in criminal, jurisdiction over mixed delicts is not cumulative, but proper and exclusive according to the divergent interests of each society. If the delict is substantially an offense of the spiritual order, but adversely affects also the civil welfare, as a heresy which is simultaneously anarchial in character, the heresy, *qua* heresy, remains spiritual in character and subject to the sole jurisdiction of the Church, while the heresy, as anarchism or disturbance of the peace, can be tried and punished by the civil authorities.[11] Moreover, a mixed delict, as prejudicial to, or inseparably annexed to, a contentious case of a spiritual character, e.g. adultery as the cause of separation, is restricted as such to the exclusive judgment of the Church, but may be tried and penalized with separable, temporal punishment by the State, as harmful to the public morals of the community.

Those crimes which are delicts of the mixed forum are subject to the proper, but cumulative jurisdiction of both societies, with the principle of "first arrival" prevailing in the determination of jurisdiction in individual cases.[12]

Thus when canon 1553 states that the Church has the proper and exclusive right of judging all violations of ecclesiastical laws, it is but drawing a corollary to the principle of finality which is the determining and measuring principle not only for the legislative rights of a perfect society, but also for the judicial power, in so far as judicial power is the necessary compliment and integral function which applies the law in individual cases.[13]

In further stating that the Church has the right to judge the violations of laws other than ecclesiastical, the Church neither denies nor contradicts, but rather develops, the principle of finality. It has no intention of claiming direct jurisdiction in temporal affairs as such. But all human acts, even those of a temporal character which are regulated by civil law or by the unwritten law of human nature and reason alone, have a moral quality, a substratum of justice, charity, truthfulness, and the like; in brief, a rightness or wrongness accordingly as they are in conformity or conflict with man's spiritual goal, and the order established by his Creator. All human acts are, consequently, of a mixed spiritual and temporal character. In this law in which the Church claims proper and exclusive judicial and coactive jurisdiction over the moral, or spiritual, element contained in all crimes, the Church is merely expressing the jurisdictional rights contained in the divine commission by which all spiritual matters have been committed to her care and jurisdiction. It is the

---

11 Wernz, *Ius Decretalium ad Usum Praelectionum in Scholis Textus Canonici sive Iuris Decretalium* (6 vols., Romae, 1898-1914), VI, 33-4.

12 Cans. 1553, § 2; 1554; 1568.

13 Cf. *supra*, pp. 3-5.

legislative embodiment of the doctrine taught so clearly by Innocent III in his letter, *Novit*:

> No one is to think that [in proceeding in the dispute between John of England and Philip of France] we intend to disturb or to diminish the jurisdiction or power of the illustrious King of France . . . for we do not intend to concern ourselves with the issues involved in the feud which pertain to his judgment . . . but to investigate concerning the commission of sin, whose censure pertains, without doubt, to us, and which we can and must exercise towards everyone . . . No one of sound mind is ignorant that it is our duty to correct every Christian for any mortal sin whatsoever, and if he shows contempt for our correction, to bring force upon him by means of ecclesiastical judicial action. [14]

The Church, then, with its divine mission of sanctification and salvation, has a direct, proper, and exclusive jurisdiction to judge, and can impose spiritual penalties in view of the violated moral element inherent in every delict, whether spiritual, temporal, or mixed.[15]

The exercise of this jurisdiction, however, is restricted by the self-imposed restraint of the Church, for in regard to public morals, the Church regularly refrains from exercising its proper jurisdiction whenever the defendant is a layman, and whenever the civil magistrate in judging such cases takes sufficient steps to safeguard the public welfare.[16] If, however, the nature of even a civil delict is such that it endangers the spiritual order and society in a way that cannot effectively be remedied through the judicial actions of the State, the Church has the right and duty to judge and punish the crime. Such a case might occur when a supposedly stalwart Catholic is convicted by the State of political graft and corruption. Not only does his crime scandalize Catholics and non-Catholics alike, but the silence or failure on the part of the Church to publicly rebuke and punish the would-be "Catholic leader" can itself be a scandal, making

---

[14] Cf. footnote 31, p. 50, for Latin quote; pp. 53-4.

[15] John, 20:21-3; Matthew, 16:19; 18:18; II *Corinthians*, 5:18.

[16] "In delictis mixti fori Ordinarii regulariter ne procedant cum reus laicus est et civilis magistratus, in reum animadvertens publico bono satis consulit."—can. 1933, § 3. "A poena infligenda abstinere, si reus perfecte fuerit emendatus, et scandalum reparavit, aut sufficienter poenis auctoritate civili sancitis."—can. 2223, § 3, 2°.

it appear that the Church is failing in its divine mission of championing the cause of morality.[17]

If the Church rarely and reluctantly uses its judicial power over temporal crimes, this is due to the high stage of development reached by the modern State, which provides due recourse for all torts and adequately defends the public morality and welfare in temporal and mixed delicts. The foremost motive behind this policy of the Church, however, is that, since its primary interest is the sanctification of souls, it prefers to treat such delicts as sins exclusively within the sacramental forum whenever this is possible. There hearts may be touched by grace, and the very willingness of the Church to deal secretly and privately with such violations assists in spiritual conversions, the indirect effect of which upon the social order is beneficial beyond the capacity of any social institution to achieve, since it would be necessary here to work without the willing co-operation of the judged.[18]

---

[17] Cf. Marchesi, *Summula Iuris Publici Ecclesiastici,* n. 65.

[18] Ottaviani, *Compendium,* n. 91.

Chapter VIII

THE JUDICIAL POWER OF THE CHURCH IN REGARD TO THE STATUS OF PERSONS

A. *General Principles*

Judicial jurisdiction depends not only on the spiritual nature or character of the matter to be judged, but upon the personages involved. If a person is not bound to the observance of a law, he cannot violate it. Therefore, the judicial power of any society is restricted to those who are subjects of its legislative power.

Saint Paul applied this restriction to the judicial power of the Church, saying, "What have I to do with judging those outside? Is it not those inside whom you judge? For those outside God will judge," [1] and Pius XII, stated, "The faithful of God's Church, whom He has purchased with His own blood, are those upon whom the judicial activity is exercised." [2] But since a person becomes a member of the Church through baptism, all baptized persons are subject to the judicial power of the Church,[3] though their rights before the ecclesiastical tribunal may be restricted, or even lost, as penalties for their delicts.[4]

Even heretics and schismatics who are validly baptised, and so are marked with the indelible, sacramental character of Christ upon their souls, remain subject to the judicial authority of the Church.[5] The Church, however, does not always exercise its full rights over

---

[1] *I Corinthians,* 5:9-13.

[2] Pius XII, Allocution to the Sacred Roman Rota, Oct. 29, 1947—*AAS,* XXXIX (1947), 497; Bouscaren, *The Canon Law Digest* Supplement through 1948, p. 218.

[3] "Baptismate homo constituitur in Ecclesia Christi persona cum omnibus christianorum iuribus et officiis, nisi ad iura quod attinet, obstet obex, ecclesiasticae communionis vinculum impediens, vel lata ab Ecclesia censura." —Can. 87.

[4] Cans. 2263; 1654; 1628, § 3; 1554.

[5] Cf. Cavagnis, *op. cit.,* I, nos. 563-4.

these people, but treats those who are formal heretics differently from those who are material heretics, and those who have already rebelled against the Church differently from those who are about to fall away from the Church. Before the rebellion or defection the Church can, and often must, exercise all its judicial rights in order to prevent the perversion of a Christian people. This duty becomes more grave proportionately to the seriousness and extent of the danger. This duty could be especially pressing when it concerned the leaders of a people, as Henry VIII, Elizabeth, or the German Princes. After the rebellion, the heretics and schismatics, as individuals or as illicit spiritual societies, are still subject to the Church in consequence of their Christian baptism, and by the will of Christ who founded one, holy, catholic, and apostolic Church as the necessary means, and the legitimate authority, for the salvation of all men.

It does not matter that the heretics are such in but a material fashion for the reason that they are distant descendants of those who formally rebelled against the Church. Time alone is no basis upon which to claim exemption from the authority from God, nor can the tolerance of the Church ever be interpreted as a recognition of the legitimacy of the juridic status of heretics or schismatics, either as individuals, or as societies. In practice, however, the Church, as a matter of prudence and charity, does not insist upon its full rights in regard to those individuals who have fallen away from the Church, lest even greater spiritual harm prevail. In judicial matters, then, they are assimilated to the non-baptized.[6]

The Church claims no jurisdiction over the non-baptized,[7] although *de iure* and objectively all men, as creatures of God, are subject to their Creator and to His will in all things, spiritual and temporal.[8] Infidels, however, may at times become indirectly subject to the Church, as through their relationship with persons and connection with cases which belong to the Church as a spiritual matter. This occurs most frequently in marriage cases in which the

[6] Cf. Cappello, *op. cit.*, nos. 260-1.

[7] "Legibus mere ecclesiasticis non tenentur qui baptismum non receperunt." —Can. 12.

[8] Innocentius IV, *Commentaria ad* c. 8, X, *de voto et voti redemptione,* III, 34; cf. *supra,* p. 44, for quote.

non-baptized person is a party to an indivisible, sacred, bilateral contract with a baptized person.[9]

The Church gives due recognition to the rights which the State holds over the faithful who are simultaneously citizens in the civil society. It claims no jurisdiction over them in temporal matters as long as the State adequately fulfills its normal duties.[10]

The special interest taken and jurisdiction exercised at times in favor of the unfortunate, such as the widows, the orphans, and the poor, the Church has not claimed as direct and exclusive, but rather as indirect and cumulative, depending on the inability of these people to gain justice in the civil courts, with the resultant harm and disorder to both the spiritual and temporal orders.[11]

B. *The Privilege of the Forum*

There is, however, a class of people, namely, the clergy and the religious, over whom, because of their peculiar spiritual character, the Church claims proper and exclusive jurisdiction, in both criminal and contentious matters. The right, which these people enjoy, to be subject to the ecclesiastical courts to the exclusion of the civil, is called the privilege of the forum.[12]

Specifically, the privilege of the forum means that the clergy and the religious can be summoned as defendants only before the ecclesiastical judges to the exclusion of the civil courts, whether the case be contentious or criminal in nature, unless the consent of the proper ecclesiastical authority be obtained either in individual cases, or as a general norm for particular places.[13]

---

[9] Cf. Benedictus XIV, const. *Singulare Nobis,* Feb. 9, 1749—*Fontes,* n. 928, in which the Pope denies the authority of the State over a mixed marriage between a Christian and a Jew; Goldsmith, *op. cit.,* pp. 46-54.

[10] Can. 1933, § 3: "In delictis mixti fori Ordinarii regulariter ne procedant cum reus laicus est et civilis magistratus, in rerum animadvertens, publico bono satis consulet."

[11] Lega-Bartoccetti, *op. cit.,* I, 16; cf. *supra,* pp. 46-7.

[12] Can. 1553, § 1, 3°.

[13] "§ 1. Clerici in omnibus causis sive contentiosis sive criminalibus apud iudicem ecclesiasticum conveniri debent, nisi aliter pro locis particularibus legitime provisum fuerit.

§ 2. Patres Cardinales, Legati Sedis Apostolicae, Episcopi etiam titulares, Abbates vel Praelati *nullius,* supremi religionum iuris pontificii Superiores,

This privilege is not primarily concerned with spiritual cases which already pertain to the judicial power of the Church by reason of their nature, even if they concern only laymen, nor with cases which might arise from the exercise of the spiritual functions of the clergy, for these are already spiritual by reason of their finality, but with any personal matters of a temporal nature in which a cleric or a religious might become involved.[14] It does not preclude the summoning of clerics and religious as witnesses in a trial, but this is often prohibited by the moral law, or by canon 119, which demands respect and reverence for the clergy.[15]

If any layman or cleric wishes to bring suit against a cleric or a religious in the civil courts, he must obtain permission from the proper ecclesiastical superior.[16] This permission should not be denied, especially when the plaintiff is a layman, except for just and grave cause, and when no settlement can be reached outside of court by agreement or arbitration.[17]

If a cleric or a religious is summoned contrary to the prescriptions of canon law, he may answer the summons, and appear in court through necessity and in order to prevent further harm, but he must inform the superior from whom the permission should have been obtained.[18]

Officiales maiores Romanae Curiae, ob negotia ad ipsorum munus pertinentia, apud iudicem laicum conveniri nequeunt sine venia Sedis Apostolicae; ceteri privilegio fori gaudentes, sine venia Ordinarii loci in quo causa peragitur; quam tamen licentiam Ordinarius, praesertim cum actor est laicus, ne deneget sine iusta et gravi causa, tum maxime cum controversiae inter partes componendae frustra operam dederit."—Can. 120.

[14] Cf. Coronata, *Institutiones Iuris Canonici,* I, n. 183.

[15] Coronata, *op cit.,* IV, n. 1973.

[16] Can. 120, § 2.

[17] Concerning extra-judicial settlements cf. cans. 1925-32. These settlements are made with due recognition for the civil laws governing the controverted matter. Criminal cases, contentious cases concerning the dissolution of a marriage, or concerning the title of benefices without the legitimate approval of the proper authority, and spiritual matters requiring the payment of temporal goods, cannot be settled outside the ecclesiastical or civil court, as can controversies concerning temporal ecclesiastical goods and the things which are separably annexed to the spiritual.

[18] Can. 120, § 3.

Those who enjoy this privilege are the clerics,[19] the religious,[20] and the persons who belong to societies in which the members do not profess public vows,[21] whether they be lay persons, or only novices.[22]

The privilege is acquired, accordingly, through the ceremony of first tonsure,[23] or through the ceremony by which one begins the novitiate, generally by receiving the religious habit.[24] Hence the privilege does not obtain for postulants, nor does it hold for crimes committed before entry in the novitiate, for the very threat or danger of criminal prosecution for a serious delict invalidates the noviceship,[25] and also the consequent religious profession of the criminal.[26] Involvement in contentious trials affects the lawfulness but not the validity, of the noviceship. Should such a case occur in spite of the precautionary investigations of the superior, the novice is clothed in ecclesiastical immunity, and the contentious matter becomes reserved to the ecclesiastical forum.[27]

The privilege of the forum is lost by a cleric through his reduction to the lay state, or through his deprivation of the clerical garb,[28] and by a religious, as a religious, through secularization,[29] or in consequence of any apostasy from the society,[30] but not by way of exclaustration.[31]

Those who presumptuously force a cleric or a religious to appear as a defendant before a civil judge are punished according to the penalties specified in canon 2341, which states that, if one dare to cite before a lay judge one of the Cardinals, Legates of the Apostolic

---

19 Can. 120, § 1.

20 Can. 614.

21 Can. 680.

22 Can. 614.

23 Can. 108, § 1.

24 Can. 553.

25 Can. 542, 1°.

26 Can. 572, § 1.

27 Can. 542, 2°.

28 Cans. 123; 136, § 3; 213; 2304.

29 Can. 640.

30 Can. 2385.

31 Can. 639. Cf. Schaefer, *De Religiosis ad Normam Codicis Iuris Canonici* (4. ed., Romae: Apostolato Cattolico, 1947), pp. 744-5; Roberti, *Iuris Processualis Compendium,* pp. 29-30.

See, or major officials of the Roman Curia in affairs pertaining to their office, or one's own proper Ordinary, one incurs automatically an excommunication reserved in a special manner to the Apostolic See; if one cites another bishop—even a titular bishop, abbot, or prelate *nullius*—or the supreme superior of any religious institute of pontifical approval, one automatically incurs an excommunication reserved simply to the Apostolic See; if a cleric without a previous permission from the local Ordinary cites before a lay judge any other person who enjoys the privilege of the forum, he automatically incurs a suspension from office reserved to the Ordinary; if a lay person commits this offense, he shall be punished by the proper Ordinary with suitable penalties in proportion to the attendant guilt.[32]

The penalty is incurred only by those who know that the defendant is a cleric, that clerics enjoy the privilege of the forum, and that the summoning of a cleric before a civil judge is subject to penalty;[33] and by those who freely commit such an offense. Judges and court officials who are constrained by the law to issue such a summons do not, therefore, incur the penalty.[34]

The privilege of the forum claimed by the Church for its clergy and religious is no more than the diplomatic immunity commonly exercised among all nations, and the privilege of the military forum accorded by nations to the members of their armed services. If it is fitting for the legates of a temporal king to receive such a courtesy, how much more fitting is it for priests of God, who come among men as ambassadors of the King of Kings! If the military order, which pertains to the same temporal realm as the civilian, is nevertheless so distinct from the civil as to necessitate and merit a separate system of courts, with the correlative privilege of the forum, how much more should the Church, whose order is entirely distinct not only from the civilian, but also from the natural, order, need and merit a separate system of courts, with the correlative privilege of the forum.[35]

---

[32] Cf. Coronata, *Institutiones Iuris Canonici,* IV, nos. 1972-6.

[33] Coronata, *op. cit.,* IV, no. 1973.

[34] Woywod, *A Practical Commentary on the Code of Canon Law,* 2 vols. (8th printing, New York: Joseph Wagner Inc., 1944), II, p. 942.

[35] Billot, *Tractatus de Ecclesia Christi,* II, 135.

The privilege of the forum does not make irresponsible citizens of the clergy and the religious, who are dedicated to the love of God, and necessarily, therefore, to the love of country, and to a respect for its laws. The laws of the land continue to be the directive norms for those who enjoy the privilege of the forum, even though they are not subject to trial or penalties before the civil courts for their infraction. Should any such unfortunate event occur, the State still has at its disposition the same means it possesses with respect to diplomats and the military. A protest to the proper ecclesiastical official, the Ordinary of the diocese, or the superior of the religious, will bring proper remedial and punitive action, either through administrative or judicial procedure, and, when the conditions warrant it, in the prudent judgment of the religious superior, through permission to the civil authorities to prosecute the case. Indeed the Church insists that such permission is not to be denied without a grave and just cause, especially when it is requested by a layman.[36]

The judicial immunity of the pope[37] from all temporal jurisdiction follows as a corollary from the reverence and the respect due to the Vicar of Christ on earth. More basically, it is one of those essential means, and necessary liberties, which are proper, natural, and inalienable to the Church in its capacity of a juridically perfect society. Without it, the divine mission of the Church would be neither secure, since it would continue subject to abusive, and hostile interference from temporal magistrates, nor stable, inasmuch as it would be affected by political turbulence and revolution, nor acceptable to all the peoples of the world, for the reason that it could constantly be suspected as a tool for the furtherance of the political ambitions of politicians. It would entail the perversion of the divine order of things, making the spiritual subject to the material, the eternal to the temporal, the sacred to the profane.[38] Papal immunity

[36] Can. 120, § 2. Cf. Downs, *The Concept of Clerical Immunity,* The Catholic University of America Canon Law Studies, n. 126 (Washington, D. C.: The Catholic University of America Press, 1941), p. 127; Billot, *op. cit.,* II, 145.

[37] "Prima Sedes a nemine iudicatur."—Can. 1556.

[38] Cf. Coronata, *Ius Publicum Ecclesiasticum,* nos. 156-8; Downs, *op. cit.,* pp. 2-3; Billot, *op. cit.,* II, 137-43.

is, therefore, rooted in the natural divine law, and draws at least an implicit corroboration from the positive divine law.[39]

The privilege of the forum enjoyed by clerics and by religious in general does not have the same urgent necessity about it for the well-being of the Church as does the immunity of the Pope. It does not flow immediately and formally from the divine law, as being essential to the ends of the Church. Rather, it is based on the divine, proper right by which the Church can determine and regulate whatever is of concern to it as a necessary or a useful means. Formally and immediately, then, the privilege of the forum draws its origin from the positive, ecclesiastical law, which determines what is proper and fitting for the Church's clergy and religious. Remotely and secondarily it is based on the natural divine law, in so far as through the acclaim of the divine law itself the Church holds the right to make such a determination.

In reserving such cases to itself the Church did not act arbitrarily, but determined and sanctioned this immunity as 1) a corollary of the divine law, which calls for due reverence and respect towards the clergy and the religious as persons specially consecrated to God; and 2) as an application of the principle of finality through which the Church's jurisdictional rights over contentious and criminal matters are established. In this analogy, clerics and religious are assimilated to supernatural *res mixtae,* for their lives are substantially sacred, being consecrated and dedicated entirely to the worship of God and the salvation of souls, while along with their retaining of national citizenship many phases of their lives remain purely temporal in character, attended with civil obligations which are neither incompatible with the sanctity of their lives, nor revoked by the Church as far as the clergy are concerned. Through this analogy, then, the temporal aspects of the lives of the clergy are temporal, separable effects related to a supernatural substance. These are properly subject to the State, unless they have been reserved, in consequence of the prerogatives held by the Church, as a juridically perfect society.

This privilege of the clergy, then, is not a native or natural right of the clergy, as it is for the Pope, but it is an immunity, a corollary

---

[39] On the occasion when Christ explained to Peter that they were not subject to the State tax.—Matthew, 17:25.

of the divine law, which depends upon the determination of the Church for the juridical, though not necessarily for the moral, obligatory character inherent in it.

It is a privilege, not in the sense that it is a concession of the State, for that would presuppose subjection to the civil law. Actually, in the face of the determination of the Church, the State merely recognizes and respects the privilege of the form as a determination of a society of a superior order, which the State has no authority to modify or revoke without abusing the public interest and the divine order. It is a privilege, in the broader sense, that certain persons are not subject to the civil tribunal by positive ecclesiastical law, which has its roots deep in the natural divine law.[40]

The ability of custom to abrogate or derogate the privilege of the forum offers difficulties on two scores, for a custom can obtain legal force only if it is reasonable in nature,[41] and if it has the consent of the legitimate authority.[42]

The doubts concerning the reasonableness of such a custom contrary to the law of privileged forum present a difficult, but not an insurmountable obstacle. In the light of the prevailing opinion that the privilege of the forum is formally of ecclesiastical rather than

---

[40] This is the thesis of Downs, *The Concept of Clerical Immunity,* who studies and rejects the theories that clerical immunity is based on the concession of the State, on formal divine law, or on positive ecclesiastical law alone. Though there is a great deal of divergence in terminology, the opinion that the privilege of the forum derives formally from positive ecclesiastical law, and remotely from the natural divine law, seems the common and more acceptable doctrine among theologians and jurists today. Cf. also, Ottaviani, *Compendium,* n. 92; Coronata, *Jus Publicum Ecclesiasticum,* nos. 150-3; Cappello, *Summa Juris Publici Ecclesiastici,* nos. 362-3; Billot, *Tractatus* de *Ecclesia Christi,* II, 135-6; 143-5.

[41] "§ 1. Iuri divino sive naturali sive positivo nulla consuetudo potest aliquatenus derogare; sed neque iuri ecclesiastico praeiudicium affert, nisi fuerit rationabilis et legitime per annos quadraginta continuos et completos praescripta; contra legem vero ecclesiasticam quae clausulam contineat futuras conseutudines prohibentem, sola praescribere potest rationabilis conseutudo centenaria aut immemorabilis.

§ 2. Consuetudo quae in iure expresse reprobatur, non est rationabilis." —can. 27.

[42] "Consuetudo in Ecclesia vim legis a consensu competentis Superioris ecclesiastici unice obtinet."—can. 25.

divine law, the objection that this custom is opposed to natural or positive divine law fails. Furthermore, the acts of the Holy See admitting the force of such customs in certain instances, and the willingness of canon 120 to allow for contrary provisions in particular places,[43] inescapably leads to the conclusion that not all cases are to be judged as so violently injurious to the discipline, authority, and welfare of the Church as to make them legally unreasonable.[44]

Moreover, from the fact that the Holy See has admitted the force of custom in some countries, as in Germany, Belgium, and Holland,[45] it is to be admitted that, in spite of the lack of reverence and the hostility which would seem to motivate such practices, and thus to force the conclusion that the silence of the legitimate authorities is not consent, but simple toleration motivated by the fear of greater evil, legal consent does sometimes exist.

On the other hand, such consent is not to be presumed too readily. In the United States, for instance, the Second and Third Councils of Baltimore, under threat of ecclesiastical penalties, forbade clerics and religious to sue other clerics and religious in the civil courts, but maintained a discreet silence concerning the obligations of laymen in this matter.[46] Even after the Motu Proprio, *"Quantavis diligentia,"* of Pius X in 1911, Ayrinhac maintained that the custom contrary to clerical immunity still prevailed.[47] But contrary to all this, the Sacred Congregation of the Council declared in a case in 1928 that certain laymen in Rhode Island had incurred the penalties established in the Code for bringing their Bishop into civil court as defendant regard-

---

[43] § 1 ". . . nisi aliter pro locis particularibus legitime provisum fuerit."

[44] For an excellent historical study of the force of custom contrary to immunity cf. Downs, *op. cit.*, pp. 42-51.

[45] Pius X, Motu Proprio, *Quantavis Diligentia,* Oct. 11, 1911—*Fontes,* n. 694.

[46] Concilii Plenarii Baltimorensis II, Acta et Decreta, ed. altera mendis expurgata (Baltimora, 1894), nos. 155-6, pp. 96-7; Concilii Plenarii Baltimorensis III, Acta et Decreta (Baltimora, 1884), n. 84, p. 45.

[47] Cf. Ayrinhac, *Penal Legislation in the New Code of Canon Law* (New York: Benziger Brothers, 1920), n. 541; *The American Ecclesiastical Review*: "Clerics and secular tribunals," XLVI (1911), 175-9; "The motu proprio *"Quantavis Diligentia,"* XLVII (1912), 303-15; "Clerics before the civil tribunal," XLVII (1912), 357-9; Downs, *op. cit.*, pp. 48-9; Coronata, *Institutiones Iuris Canonici,* IV, nos. 1972-3.

ing official acts, thus making it evident that such a custom does not prevail against the law in the United States.[48]

Thus, while admitting that customs contrary to the privilege of the forum can now be admitted to exist in some restricted instances, it can not be held as a general principle that the permission necessary to summon a cleric or religious as defendant before the civil courts can be neglected on the plea of contrary custom.

---

[48] *AAS,* XX (1928), p. 146; Ayrinhac, new revised edition of Penal Legislation in the New Code of Canon Law, by Lydon, 1936.

CONCLUSIONS

I. The judicial power of the Church is "proper and exclusive" in its origins because it is founded on the positive divine law (Matthew, 18:15-18), and on the divinely willed status of the Church as a necessary, juridically perfect society, from which judicial power flows as a corollary to the native right of juridically perfect societies to all the means necessary to the accomplishment of their ends. It is a truly jurisdictional power, because, being based on the positive divine law, it is not the product of the free, mutual consent of the members of the society, but derives its obligatory character from outside the human will.

II. The theories which regard the judicial power of the Church as rooted solely in the natural law do not offer the true basis for the judicial rights of the Church.

III. Nevertheless, in nations where the commingling of Catholic and non-Catholic citizens makes it impractical for the State to recognize the divine authority of the Church as such, it is legitimate for the State to view the authority of the Church as a corollary of religious freedom.

IV. In considering religious rights from a purely natural standpoint, and in failing to recognize the divine authority of the Church, the State inescapably maintains for the civil law and the temporal welfare a claim that is absolute and supreme, and thus exercises a certain police power over the religious activities of its subjects.

V. The Church, however, has little to fear, in practice, from the exercise of such a police power when it is exercised by a State which truly respects the natural law and the rights of conscience.

VI. If the Church has every right to expect that, given the good will of the State, such a system will provide an ample working basis upon which to carry out its divine mission, the State can be even more confident that the judicial activities of the Church will blend harmoniously with the peace and order of the temporal society, and the functions of the civil courts.

BIBLIOGRAPHY

SOURCES

Acta Apostolicae Sedis, Commentarium Officiale, Romae, 1909—

Bouscaren, T. Lincoln, *The Canon Law Digest,* 2 vols. and Supplement through 1948, Milwaukee: Bruce Publishing Co., Vol. I, 1934, Vol. II, 1943, Supplement, 1949.

Codex Iuris Canonici Pii X Pontificis Maximi iussu digestus, Benedicti Papae XV auctoritate promulgatus, Romae: Typis Polyglottis Vaticanis, 1917.

Codex Theodosianus, ed. P. Krueger, Berolini: apud Weidmannos, 1923-1926.

Codicis Iuris Canonici Fontes, cura Emi Card. Gasparri editi, 9 vols., Romae (postea, Civitate Vaticana): Typis Polyglottis Vaticanis, 1923-1939 (Vols. VII-IX, ed. cura et studio Emi Iustiniani Card. Seredi).

Concilii Plenarii Baltimorensis II, Acta et Decreta, ed. altera mendis expurgata, Baltimorae, 1894.

Concilii Plenarii Baltimorensis III, Acta et Decreta, Baltimorae, 1884.

Corpus Iuris Canonici, editio Lipsiensis secunda post Aemilii Ludovici Richteri curas instruxit Aemilius Friedburg, 1879-1881. Editio anastatice repetita, Lipsiae: Tauchnitz, 1928.

Corpus Iuris Civilis, 3 vols., Berolini: apud Weidmannos, 1928-1929; Vol. II, *Codex Iustinianus,* ed. stereotypa decima, recognovit et rectractavit P. Krueger; Vol. III, *Novellae,* ed. stereotypa quinta quas recognovit R. Schoell, et absolvit G. Kroll.

Decretales D. Gregorii Papae IX suae integritati una cum glossis restitutae, cum privilegio Gregorii XIII, Pont. Max., et aliorum Principum, Romae, 1582.

Enchiridion Symbolorum Definitionum et Declarationum de Rebus Fidei et Morum, ed. H. Denzinger, C. Bannwart, J. Umberg, 21-23 ed., Friburgi Brisgoviae: Herder & Co., 1937.

Hardouin, Jean, *Acta Conciliorum et Epistolae Decretales ac Constitutiones Summorum Pontificum,* 12 vols., Parisiis, 1714-1715.

Innocentius IV, *Commentaria in V Libros Decretalium,* Venetiis, 1552.

Jaffé, Phillipus, *Regesta Pontificum Romanorum ab condita Ecclesia ad annum post Christum natum MCXCVIII,* 2. ed. correctam et auctam auspiciis Gulielmi Wattenbach, curaverunt S. Löwenfeld, F. Kaltenbrunner, P. Ewald, 2 vols., Lipsiae, 1885-1888.

Mansi, Joannes D., *Sacrorum Conciliorum Nova et Amplissima Collectio,* 53 vols. in 60, Parisiis, Arnhem, Lipsiae, 1901-1927.

Migne, J. P., *Patrologiae Cursus Completus, Series Graeca,* 161 vols., Parisiis, 1857-1866.

———, *Patrologiae Cursus Completus, Series Latina,* 221 vols., Parisiis, 1844-1855.

Potthast, A., ***Regesta Pontificum,*** 2 vols., Berolini, 1874-1875.

Schroeder, H. J., ***Canons and Decrees of the Council of Trent,*** St. Louis: B. Herder Co., 1941.

REFERENCE WORKS

Alzog, John, ***Manual of Universal Church History,*** translated by Pabisch and Byrne in 3 vols., Cincinnati, Ohio, 1874.

Aquinas, Thomas, St., ***Summa Theologica,*** 5 vols., Taurini: Marietti, 1932.

Ayrinhac, H. A., S.S., ***Penal Legislation in the New Code of Canon Law,*** New York: Benziger Brothers, 1920; new revised edition by P. J. Lydon, 1936.

Bellarminus, Robertus Card., S.J., ***Opera Omnia,*** 6 vols., Neapoli, 1856-1862; Parisiis, 12 vols., 1874.

Bender, Ludovicus, O.P., ***Ius Publicum Ecclesiasticum,*** Bussum in Hollandia: Paulus Brand, 1948.

Billot, Ludovico Card., S.J., ***Tractatus de Ecclesia Christi,*** 2 vols. in 1, 5. ed., Romae: apud Aedes Universitatis Gregorianae, 1927.

Bouix, D., ***Tractatus de Judiciis Ecclesiasticis,*** 3 ed., 2 vols. in 1, Parisiis, 1855.

Boyd, William K., ***The Ecclesiastical Edicts of the Theodosian Code,*** Faculty of Political Science of Columbia University, Vol. XXIV, n. 2, New York: The Columbia University Press, 1905.

Cambridge Medieval History, The, 8 vols., New York: Macmillan Co., 1911-1936.

Cambridge Summer School of Catholic Studies, 1935, ***Church and State,*** London: Burns Oates and Washbourne, Ltd., 1936.

Cappello, F., S.J., ***Summa Iuris Publici Ecclesiastici,*** 2. ed., Romae: apud Aedes Universitatis Gregorianae, 1928.

Cardozo, Benjamin N., ***Cardozo, Selected Writings,*** edited by M. Hall, New York: Fallon Book Co., 1947.

Cavagnis, F., ***Institutionis Iuris Publici Ecclesiastici,*** 4. ed., 3 vols., Romae, 1906.

Carlyle, R. W., and Carlyle, A. D., ***A History of Mediaeval Political Theory In the West,*** 6 vols., New York: Barnes and Noble Inc., 1903-1936.

Catholic Encyclopedia, The, 15 vols., Index and 2 Supplements, New York, 1907-1922.

Cicognani, Amleto Giovanni, ***Canon Law,*** 2. ed., authorized English version, revised by J. O'Hara and F. Brennan, Westminster, Maryland: The Newman Press, 1935.

————, ***Commentarium ad Primum Librum Codicis Iuris Canonici,*** Romae: ex Officina Typographica Romana "Buona Stampa," 1939.

Coleman, Christopher Bush, ***Constantine the Great and Christianity,*** New York: The Columbia University Press, 1914.

Coronata, Matthaeus Conte a, O.F.M.Cap., ***Institutiones Iuris Canonici,*** 2. ed., 5 vols., Taurini: Marietti, 1939-1947.

————, *Ius Publicum Ecclesiasticum,* 3. ed., Taurini: Marietti, 1948.

Dictionnaire de Théologie Catholique, 15 vols. in 30, with the *Tables Generales,* Paris: Libraire Letouzey et Ané, 1903-1951.

Downs, John Emmanuel, *The Concept of Clerical Immunity,* The Catholic University of America Canon Law Studies, n. 126, Washington, D. C.: The Catholic University of America Press, 1941.

Goldsmith, J. William, *The Competence of Church and State over Marriage —Disputed Points,* The Catholic University of America Canon Law Studies, n. 197, Washington, D. C.: The Catholic University of America Press, 1944.

Hayes, Carlton J., *Political and Social History of Modern Europe,* 2 vols., New York: Macmillan, 1920.

Hergenröther, Joseph, *Catholic Church and Christian State,* 2 vols. in 1, London, 1876.

Hughes, Philip, *A History of the Church,* 3 vols., New York: Sheed and Ward, 1934-1947.

Hull, Robert, S.J., *Medieval Theories of the Papacy and other Essays,* collected and arranged by Edmund F. Sutcliffe, S.J., London: Burns Oates and Washbourne Ltd., 1934.

Lega, Michaële Card.—Bartoccetti, Vittorio, *Commentarius in Iudicia Ecclesiastica,* 2. ed., 3 vols., Romae: Anonima Libraria Cattolica Italiana, 1950.

Lottin, Odon, Dom, *Principes de Morale,* 2 vols., Louvain: Editions de l'Abbaye de Mont Cesar, 1947.

Marchesi, Franciscus M., S.J., *Summula Iuris Publici Ecclesiastici,* Neapoli: M. D'Auria, 1948.

Messner, J., *Social Ethics,* St. Louis, Mo.: B. Herder Co., 1949.

Moulart, Ferd. J., *L'Eglise et l'Etat,* Louvain, Paris, 1887.

Ottaviani, Alaphridus, *Compendium Iuris Publici Ecclesiastici,* 2. ed., Romae: apud Custodiam Librariam Pontificii Instituti Utriusque Iuris, 1948.

————, *Institutiones Iuris Publici Ecclesiastici,* 3. ed., 2 vols., Civitate Vaticana: Typis Polyglottis Vaticanis, 1947-1948.

Plucknett, Theodore F. T., *A Concise History of the Common Law,* Rochester, New York: Lawyers Co-operative Publishing Co., 1929.

Powers, Francis J., C.S.V., *Religious Liberty and the Police Power of the State,* School of Law of the Catholic University of America, Washington, D. C.: The Catholic University of America Press, 1948.

Rager, John C., *Political Philosophy of Blessed Cardinal Bellarmine,* The Catholic University of America Theological Studies, n. 24, Shelbyville, Ind.: Quality Print Inc., 1926.

Regatillo, Eduardus F., S.J., *Institutiones Iuris Canonici,* 2 vols., Santander, 1941-1942.

Rivière, Jean, *Le Problême de l'Eglise et de l'Etat au Temps de Philippe le Bel,* Paris, Louvain: E. Champion, 1926.

Roberti, F., *Iuris Processualis Compendium,* 2 vols., Romae: apud Custodiam Librariam Instituti Utriusque Iuris, 194 ?

Schaefer, P. Timotheus, O.F.M.Cap., *De Religiosis ad Norman Codicis Iuris Canonici,* 4. ed., Roma: Editrice "Apostolato Cattolico," 1947.

Seppelt, Francis X—Löffler, Klemens, *A Short History of the Popes,* adapted from the German by Arthur Preuss, St. Louis, Mo.: B. Herder Co., 1932.

Smith, Walter Denton, *Handbook of Elementary Law,* Hornbrook Series, St. Paul, Minn.: West Publishing Co., 1939.

Smith, William, Sir, *A Dictionary of Christian Antiquities,* 2 vols., Hartford, 1880.

Stokes, Anson Phelps, *Church and State in the United States,* 3 vols., New York: Harper & Brothers, 1950.

Suarez, Francisco, S.J., *Selections from Three Works of Francisco Suarez,* Carnegie Endowment for International Peace, 2 vols.: photographic reproduction and English translation, New York: The Oxford Press, Oxford: The Clarendon Press, 1944.

Tanquerey, A., *Synopsis Theologiae Dogmaticae Fundamentalis,* 24. ed., Parisiis, Tornaci (Belg.), Romae: J. B. Bord, Typis Societatis Sancti Joannis Evangelistae, 1938.

Torpey, William George, *Judicial Doctrines of Religious Rights in America,* Chapel Hill: The University of North Carolina Press, 1948.

Ullmann, Walter, *Medieval Papalism,* London: Methuen & Co., 1949.

Van Hove, A., *Prolegomena ad Codicem Iuris Canonici,* 2. ed., Mechliniae, Romae: H. Dessain, 1945.

Vermeersch, A., S.J.—Creusen, J., S.J., *Epitome Juris Canonici,* 3 vols., Vol. I, 7. ed., 1949; Vol. II, 6. ed., 1940; Vol. III, 6. ed., 1946; Mechliniae, Romae: H. Dessain.

Wernz, F. X., *Ius Decretalium ad Usum Praelectionum in Scholis Textus Canonici sive Iuris Decretalium,* 6 vols., Romae, 1898-1914.

Wernz-Vidal, *Ius Canonicum ad Codicis Normam Exactum,* 7 vols. in 9, Romae: apud Aedes Universitatis Gregorianae, 1923-1938.

Woywod, Stanislaus, *A Practical Commentary on the Code of Canon Law,* 2 vols., 8th printing, New York: Joseph Wagner Inc., 1944.

Zollmann, Carl, *American Civil Church Law,* Faculty of Political Science of Columbia University, Vol. 77, New York: Longmans, Green & Co., 1917.

ARTICLES

Amann, E., "Optat de Milève, Saint," *Dictionnaire de Théologie Catholique,* XIII, cols. 1077-84.

Godet, P., "Gélase," *Dictionnaire de Thèologie Catholique,* VI, cols. 1182-3.

Myers, Edward, "Gelasius of Cyzicus," *Catholic Encyclopedia,* VI, 407.

Phillimore, Walter, G. P., "Discipline," *A Dictionary of Christian Antiquities,* I, 566-8.

————, "Jurisdiction," *A Dictionary of Christian Antiquities,* I, 894-8.

Fenton, Joseph Clifford, "Principles Underlying Traditional Church-State Doctrine," *The American Ecclesiastical Review,* CXXVI (June 1952), pp. 452-62; cf. also May 1953.

PERIODICALS

American Ecclesiastical Review, The (later: *The Ecclesiastical Review*), Philadelphia, 1899—

Catholic Mind, The, New York: The America Press, 1903—

ABBREVIATIONS

AAS—Acta Apostolicae Sedis

Bouscaren—*Canon Law Digest*

Can.—Canon of the *Codex Iuris Canonici*

Carnegie, *Selections*—Carnegie Endowment for International Peace, *Selections from Three Works of Francisco Suarez*

C. Iust.—Codex Iustinianus

C. Th.—Codex Theodosianus

Denzinger—*Enchiridion Symbolorum Definitionum et Declarationum de Rebus Fidei et Morum*

Fontes—Codicis Iuris Canonici Fontes

Innocentius III—*Regesta* (*MPL,* vols. 24-216. Numbered according to the year of pontificate)

Innocentius IV—Commentaria—*Commentaria in V libros Decretalium*

Mansi—*Sacrorum Conciliorum Nova et Amplissima Collectio*

MPG—Migne, *Patrologia, Series Graeca*

MPL—Migne, *Patrologia, Series Latina*

Mediaeval Political Theory—Carlyle and Carlyle, *A History of Mediaeval Political Theory in the West*

Ottaviani, *Compendium—Compendium Iuris Publici Ecclesiastici*

Plucknett, *Common Law—A Concise History of the Common Law*

Suarez, *Defensio Fidei—Defensio Fidei Catholicae et Apostolicae Adversus Anglicanae Sectae Errores*

BIOGRAPHICAL NOTE

Rev. John Rohan Bourque was born in Holyoke, Massachusetts, March 22, 1924. He attended the local public schools, and received his training in the classics at Holy Cross College, Worcester, Mass. In 1943 he entered the Seminary of Philosophy in Montreal, and the Grand Seminary of Montreal two years later. He received his Licentiate in Sacred Theology in June, 1948, and was ordained by the Most Reverend Thomas M. O'Leary, Bishop of Springfield, on December 18, 1948. Following his ordination he served as an assistant at Holy Name Church, Springfield. In the fall of 1950 he was assigned by the Most Reverend Christopher J. Weldon, the newly consecrated Bishop of Springfield, for studies in the School of Canon Law at the Catholic University of America. There he received the Baccalaureate in Canon Law in June, 1951, and the Licentiate in Canon Law in June, 1952.

ALPHABETICAL INDEX

CANON LAW STUDIES *

337. Bourque, Rev. John R., S.T.L., J.C.L., The judicial power of the Church—Canon 1553, § 1
338. Cornell, Rev. Charles E., A.B., S.T.B., J.C.L., The juridical status of heretics and schismatics in good faith
339. Fitzgerald, Rev. William Francis, A.B., S.T.L., J.C.L., The parish census and the *liber status animarum*
340. Kubik, Rev. Stanislaus J., S.T.D., J.C.L., Invalidity of dispensations according to canon 84, § 1
341. Nugent, Rev. John Gerard, C.M., J.C.L., Ordination in societies of the common life
342. Peterson, Rev. Casimir Melvyn, S.S., A.B., S.T.L., J.C.L., Spiritual care in diocesan seminaries
343. Reiss, Rev. John Charles, A.B., S.T.L., J.C.L., The time and place of sacred ordination
344. Sheehan, Rev. Joseph G., J.C.L., The obligation of respect and obedience of clerics to their ordinary—Canon 127
345. Shekleton, Rev. Matthew M., O.S.M., J.C.L., Doctrinal interpretation of law
346. Viau, Rev. Roger, S.T.L., J.C.L., Doubt in Canon Law
347. Walsh, Rev. Donnell Anthony, A.B., J.C.L., The new law on secular institutes

* For a complete list of available numbers of this series apply to the Catholic University of America Press, 620 Michigan Avenue, N. E., Washington (17), D. C.

www.ingramcontent.com/pod-product-compliance
Lightning Source LLC
LaVergne TN
LVHW050221080826
844660LV00012B/448

* 9 7 8 0 8 1 3 2 2 5 0 7 4 *